Special Locations

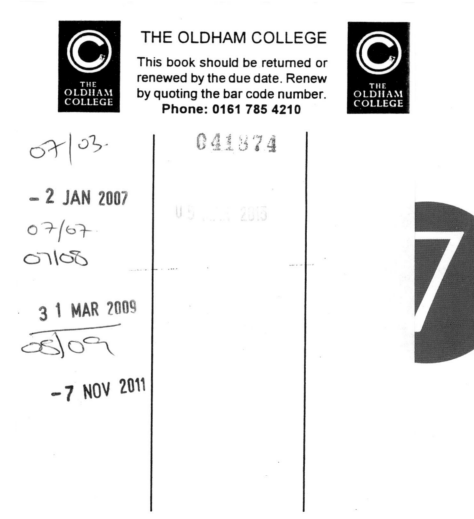

IEE Wiring Regulations

7 BS 7671 : 2001 Requirements for Electrical Installations
Including Amd No 1 : 2002

Published by: The Institution of Electrical Engineers, Savoy Place, LONDON, United Kingdom, WC2R 0BL

©2003: The Institution of Electrical Engineers, London

Issued April 1998
2nd edition incorporating Amendment No 1 to BS 7671 : 2001

Copies may be obtained from:

The IEE
PO Box 96, STEVENAGE,
United Kingdom. SG1 2SD

Tel: +44 (0)1438 767 328
Fax: +44 (0)1438 742 792
Email: sales@iee.org
http://www.iee.org/publish/books/WireAssoc//

ISBN 0 85296 995 3, 2003

Contents

Co-operating Organisations

The Institution of Electrical Engineers acknowledges the contribution made by the following organisations in the preparation of this Guidance Note.

Association of Manufacturers of Domestic Appliances
    S A MacConnacher BSc CEng MIEE

British Cables Association
    C K Reed I Eng MIIE

British Electrotechnical & Allied Manufacturers Association Ltd
    R Lewington Associate IEE

British Electrotechnical Approvals Board
    P D Stokes MA CEng MRAeS

British Standards Institution
    M Danvers

City & Guilds of London Institute
    H R Lovegrove IEng FIIE

Department of Trade and Industry
    G Scott BEng ACGI MSc CEng FIIE

Electrical Contractors' Association
    D Locke IEng MIIE ACIBSE

Electrical Contractors' Association of Scotland t/a SELECT
    D Millar IEng MIIE MILE

Electrical Installation Equipment Manufacturers' Association Ltd
    Eur Ing M H Mullins BA CEng MIEE FIIE

Electricity Association Limited
    D J Start BSc CEng MIEE

ERA Technology Ltd
    M W Coates B Eng

Federation of the Electronics Industry
    F W Pearson CEng MIIE

The GAMBICA Association Ltd
    K A Morriss BSc CEng MIEE MInstMC

Health & Safety Executive
    Eur Ing J A McLean BSc(Hons) CEng FIEE FIOSH

Institution of Electrical Engineers
    P Cook CEng FIEE MCIBSE - editor
    P E Donnachie BSc CEng FIEE
    D W M Latimer CEng FIEE MA

Institution of Incorporated Engineers
    P Tootill IEng MIIE

Lighting Association
    K R Kearney IEng MIIE

National Caravan Council Ltd
    J Lally B Eng

National Inspection Council for Electrical Installation Contracting

NHS Scotland
    M H Al-Rufaie BSc MIEE FIHEEM

Safety Assessment Federation Limited
    J Gorman BSc(Hons) CEng MIEE

Society of Electrical and Mechanical Engineers serving Local Government
    C Tanswell CEng MIEE MCIBSE

Acknowledgements

References to British Standards, CENELEC Harmonisation Documents and International Electrotechnical Committee standards are made with the kind permission of BSI. Complete copies can be obtained by post from:

BSI Customer Services
389 Chiswick High Road
London   W4 4AL

Tel: General Switchboard: 020 8996 9000
       For ordering: 020 8996 9001
       For information or advice: 020 8996 7111
       For membership: 020 8996 7002

Fax: For orders: 020 8996 7001
       For information or advice: 020 8996 7048

BSI operates an export advisory service — Technical Help to Exporters — which can advise on the requirements of foreign laws and standards. The BSI also maintains stocks of international and foreign standards, with many English translations.

Up-to-date information on BSI standards can be obtained from the BSI website, http://www.bsi-global.com/

Figure 11.1 is reproduced from NJUG Publication No 7 with the kind permission of:

The National Joint Utilities Group (NJUG)
30 Millbank
London   SW1P 4RD
Tel: 020 7963 5720   Fax: 020 7963 5989

from whom complete copies of the recommended positioning of utilities, mains and plants for new works and other publications can be obtained.

Figure 11.2 is reproduced from the Institution of Lighting Engineers Code of Practice for Electrical Safety:

Institution of Lighting Engineers
Regent House
Rugby CV21 2PN
Tel: 01788 576 492   Fax: 01788 540 145

Preface

This Guidance Note is part of a series issued by the Wiring Regulations Policy Committee of the Institution of Electrical Engineers to simplify some of the requirements of BS 7671 : 2001 inc Amd No 1, Requirements for Electrical Installations (IEE Wiring Regulations Sixteenth Edition). Significant changes made in this 2nd edition of the Guidance Note are sidelined.

Note this Guidance Note does not ensure compliance with BS 7671. It is a simple guide to some of the requirements of BS 7671 but users of these Guidance Notes should always consult BS 7671 to satisfy themselves of compliance.

The scope includes not only those special installations or locations included in BS 7671, but also

Chapter 9	Marinas
Chapter 10	Medical locations
Chapter 12	Photovoltaic power systems
Chapter 13	Exhibitions, shows and stands
Chapter 14	Floor and ceiling heating systems
Chapter 15	Extra-low voltage lighting
Chapter 16	Gardens
Chapter 17	Mobile and transportable units
Chapter 18	Small scale embedded generators (SSEG)

The Health and Safety Executive have advised that installations which conform to the standards laid down in BS 7671 are regarded by them as likely to achieve conformity with the relevant parts of the Electricity at Work Regulations 1989. However, designers and installers must always attempt to anticipate the special risks associated with any particular installation that might require precautions additional to or different from those described in BS 7671 and in this Guidance Note in order to comply with relevant legislation.

Users of this Guidance Note should assure themselves that they have complied with any legislation that post-dates the publication.

Introduction

General

This Guidance Note provides advice on the special installations and locations of Part 6 of BS 7671, Requirements for Electrical Installations, and the special installations and locations for which the International Electrotechnical Committee (IEC) have published requirements.

It is to be noted that BS 7671 and this Guidance Note are concerned with the design, selection, erection, inspection and testing of electrical installations and that these documents may need to be supplemented by the requirements or recommendations of other British Standards. Other standards of note are described in Regulation 110-01-01, including BS EN 60079 and BS EN 50014 for electrical apparatus for use in potentially explosive atmospheres (other than mining applications or explosive processing and manufacture) and BS EN 50281 for electrical apparatus with protection by enclosure for use in the presence of combustible dusts.

Part 6 of BS 7671 supplements or modifies the general requirements contained in the remainder of the standard. Thus particular protective measures may not be allowed or supplementary measures may be required. Exceptionally, for street lighting, certain requirements are relaxed. However, it is important to remember that in the absence of any comment or requirement in Part 6, then the relevant requirements of the rest of the Regulations are to be applied.

In certain of the general regulations there is a note that a particular protective measure shall not be used in particular circumstances. Regulation 471-08-01 advises that for installations and locations of increased shock risk, such as those in Part 6, additional measures (and these are in no preferred order of priority) may be required, such as the use of RCDs, supplementary bonding or reduced disconnection times.

International and European Standards

Part 6 of BS 7671 technically aligns with the relevant CENELEC Harmonization Document (HD), except for Section 601 (bathrooms) which is based on the last CENELEC draft. The preface to BS 7671 identifies the particular CENELEC Harmonization Document current at the time of publication.

For those persons engaged in work outside the UK the Guidance Note advises whether BS 7671 is based on the European (HD) or the International (IEC) standard.

Contents

The Guidance Note discusses all the sections of Part 6 and includes chapters on special locations installations not included in BS 7671 as follows:

The guidance is based on published IEC standards and draft CENELEC proposals, except for Chapter 16, Gardens.

Exclusions

110-01-01
110-02-01 The guide does not consider those special installations or equipment where the requirements are specified in other British Standards, such as:-

installations in potentially explosive atmospheres

installation of apparatus for use in the presence of combustible dusts

emergency lighting installations

fire detection and alarm systems.

Chapter 1
LOCATIONS CONTAINING A BATH OR SHOWER
Sect 601

1.1 Scope

The requirements of the section apply to locations containing baths or showers. The requirements are more specifically for bathrooms or shower rooms although there are relaxed requirements where shower cubicles only are installed in a room other than a bathroom or a shower room (most usually a bedroom).

601-01-01
601-04-02
601-08-02

The requirements do not apply to emergency facilities in industrial areas and laboratories, on the presumption that they will only be used in an emergency. Where they are used with any regularity the general requirements of the section would apply.

The requirements do not specifically apply to locations containing baths or showers for medical treatment or for disabled persons in that additional requirements or special requirements may be necessary. Guidance is given in Chapter 10 on Medical Locations.

The requirements also apply for cabinets containing a shower and/or bath .

601-01-01

1.2 The risks

The following information is provided to give a better understanding of why particular requirements are necessary for bathrooms and other wet locations.

Persons in bathrooms are particularly at risk because of a reduction of body impedance due to:
1) lack of clothing, particularly footwear
2) presence of water reducing contact resistance
3) immersion in water, reducing total body resistance
4) ready availability of earthed metal
5) increased contact area.

Clothing

Clothing can greatly increase the total body resistance, particularly insulating shoes or boots.

Body impedance

Body impedances vary from person to person and with the applied voltage, as is shown by Table 1A.

For voltages up to 50 volts, impedances with contact areas wetted with fresh water are 10 % to 25 % lower than in dry conditions. Conductive solutions can decrease the impedance considerably, to half or less of the value measured in dry conditions.

Immersion

Immersion of the body in the bath water can also significantly reduce body resistances to typically half those when not immersed, as is shown with Figure 1.1.

TABLE 1A Total body impedance Z_T for a current path hand to hand a.c. 50/60 Hz, for large surface areas of contact (note 2)

Touch voltage	Values for the total body impedance (Ω) that are not exceeded for a percentage (percentile rank) of		
V	5 % of the population	50 % of the population	95 % of the population
25	1 750	3 250	6 100
50	1 450	2 625	4 375
75	1 250	2 200	3 500
100	1 200	1 875	3 200
125	1 125	1 625	2 875
220	1 000	1 350	2 125
700	750	1 100	1 550
1 000	700	1 050	1 500
Asymptotic value	650	750	850
NOTE - Some measurements indicate that the total body impedance for the current path hand to foot is somewhat lower than for a current path hand to hand (10 % to 30 %)			

Fig 1.1 Impedances of the human body

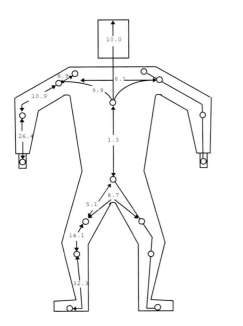

The numbers indicate the percentage of the internal impedance of the human body for the part of the body concerned, as a percentage of the path one hand to one foot.

NOTE 1 - Should it be wished to calculate the total body impedance Z_T for a given current path, the percentage internal impedances of all parts in the body of the current path have to be added to give a percentage of the value in table 1A.

NOTE 2 - Large areas of contact - exceeding 8000 mm²

from fig 2 of IEC 479-1

These reductions in body resistance and contact resistance, coupled with the ready availability of the earthed metalwork from pipes etc. make a bathroom particularly hazardous and require special precautions to be taken.

1.3   The zones

Zones 0, 1, 2 and 3 provide a very practical method of specifying requirements for protection against the ingress of water and protection against electric shock, supplementary bonding, etc in a specific and unambiguous way. Equipment is either in a zone or outside a zone and this can be determined by measurement.

The zones are determined taking account of walls, doors, fixed partitions, ceilings and floors where these effectively limit the extent of the zone. This means that a zone does not extend through a door opening (with a door) nor does it pass through a fixed partition. The zone does extend through an opening without a door (see Fig 1.2).

In the 1992 Edition of BS 7671 devices for isolation and switching were required to be so situated as to be normally inaccessible to a person using a fixed bath or shower. For practical reasons this requirement can now be considered to mean installed outside zones 0, 1 and 2, i.e. in zone 3 or outside all of the zones.

Fig: 1.2 Zones for equipment in proximity to baths and showers

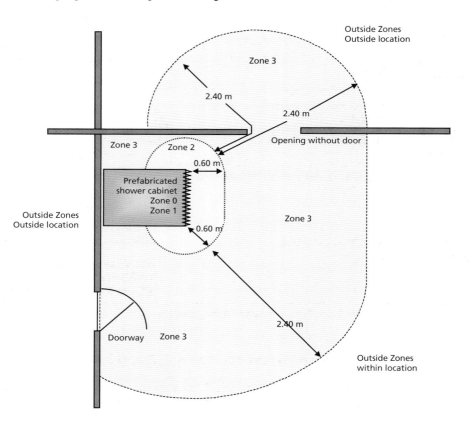

1.4   Protection against electric shock

Bathrooms and shower rooms

Disconnection times for circuits supplying current-using equipment are no longer reduced to 0.4 s. However, 30 mA RCDs are to be fitted to the circuits of certain items of current-using equipment (see Table 1B).

TABLE 1B **Requirements for equipment (current-using and accessories) in locations containing a bath or shower**

Zone note 2	Requirements for equipment in the zones		
	Minimum degree of protection	Current-using equipment e.g. appliance or luminaire	Switchgear, controlgear and accessories
0	IPX7	Only 12 V SELV fixed equipment that cannot be located elsewhere.	None allowed.
1	IPX4 (IPX5 where waterjets are liable to be used)	12 V SELV equipment allowed. Water heaters, showers, shower pumps, allowed. Other fixed equipment that cannot reasonably be located elsewhere allowed if protected by a 30 mA RCD.	Only 12 V a.c. and 30 V d.c. switches of SELV circuits allowed, the source being outside zones 0, 1 and 2.
2	IPX4 (IPX5 where waterjets are liable to be used)	SELV equipment allowed. Water heaters, showers, shower pumps, luminaires, fans, heating appliances, units for whirlpool baths allowed. Other fixed equipment that cannot reasonably be located elsewhere allowed.	SELV switches and sockets allowed, the source being outside zones 0, 1 and 2, and shaver supply units to BS EN 60742 Ch 2 Sec 1 or BS EN 61558-2-5 allowed only if fixed where direct spray from showers is unlikely.
3	No requirement	SELV equipment allowed. Current-using equipment allowed and, unless fixed, must be protected by a 30 mA RCD.	Allowed except for socket-outlets. There must be no provision for connecting portable equipment. SELV sockets and shaver supply units to BS EN 60742 Chap 2 Sect 1 or BS EN 61558-2-5 allowed.
Outside Zones	No requirement	Appliances allowed	Allowed except for socket-outlets. SELV sockets and shaver supply units to BS EN 60742 Chap 2 Sect 1 or BS EN 61558-2-5 allowed.

Note 1: See Figures 1.3 and 1.4 for zones.

PELV is allowed to be used in zones 1, 2 and 3 and outside the zones.

Socket-outlets other than SELV socket-outlets and shaver-supply units complying with BS EN 60742 Chapter 2 Section 1 or BS EN 61558-2-5 that is supplied by a safety isolating transformer, are not allowed anywhere in a bathroom or shower room whatever the size.

Fig 1.3 Supplementary bonding in a bathroom - metal pipe installation

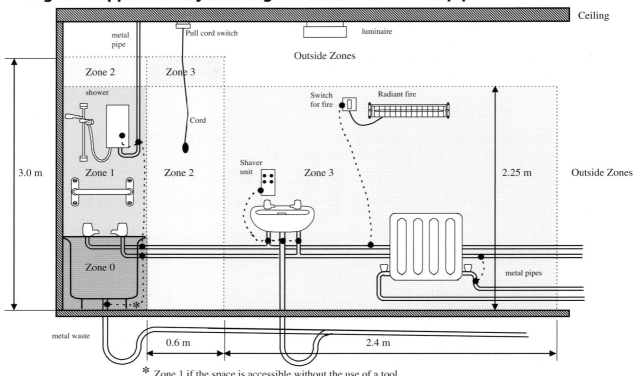

* Zone 1 if the space is accessible without the use of a tool.
Spaces under the bath, accessible only with the use of a tool, are outside the zones.

Note 1: The protective conductors of all power and lighting points within the zones must be supplementary bonded to all extraneous-conductive-parts in the zones, including metal waste, water and central heating pipes, and metal baths and metal shower basins.

Note 2: Circuit protective conductors may be used as supplementary bonding conductors.

Fig 1.4 Supplementary bonding in a bathroom - plastic pipe installation

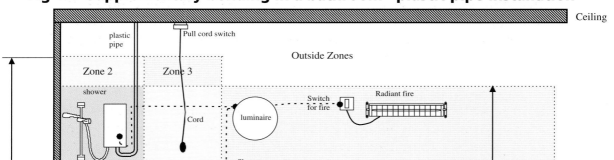

* Zone 1 if the space is accessible without the use of a tool.
Spaces under the bath, accessible only with the use of a tool, are outside the zones.

Note 1: The protective conductors of all power and lighting points within the zones must be supplementary bonded. The bonding connection may be to the earth terminal of a switch or accessory supplying equipment.

Note 2: Circuit protective conductors may be used as supplementary bonding conductors.

Other rooms containing a shower cubicle

In rooms with shower cubicles other than bathrooms or shower rooms, such as bedrooms or industrial locations, socket-outlets are allowed provided they are installed outside zones 0, 1, 2 or 3. When installed outside the zones in such locations socket-outlets are required to be protected by an RCD with a rated residual operating current $I_{\Delta n}$ not exceeding 30 mA.

601-08-02
412-06

Supplementary bonding

601-04

Supplementary bonding is required for all locations including bedrooms containing a bath or shower in zones 1 and 2 and also in zone 3 for bathrooms and shower rooms, but not outside the zones. The supplementary bonding is required to connect extraneous-conductive-parts including metal pipes, central heating, air conditioning, accessible metal structural parts of the building in contact with earth and metal baths and metal shower basins, to the protective conductors of circuits supplying equipment in the zones. For example, the supplementary bond to a luminaire circuit could be made at the luminaire or at the switch. Similarly, for shower circuits the supplementary bond from extraneous-conductive-parts could be made at the shower switch or at the shower.

601-04-02

Supplementary bonding does not necessarily have to be carried out within the bathroom itself but may be carried out in close proximity such as under the floor boards, above the ceiling, or in an adjacent airing cupboards.

601-04-01

The requirement to supplementary bond to the protective conductors of circuits supplying both Class I and Class II equipment is necessary in case during the life of the installation the user changes a Class II piece of equipment for Class I.

Supplementary bonding of plastic pipe installations

Supplementary bonding is not required to metallic parts supplied by plastic pipes such as metal hot and cold water taps supplied from plastic pipes or a metal bath not connected to extraneous-conductive-parts such as structural steelwork and where the hot and cold water pipes and the waste are plastic.

Supplementary bonding is not required to short lengths of metal pipes which are often installed for cosmetic reasons when the basic plumbing system is plastic.

1.5 Wiring systems

Metal conduit and metal trunking wiring systems are allowed in the zones of bathrooms provided they are supplementary bonded within the zones. They do not have to supply equipment within the zones.

601-07-01
522-06-07

1.6 Switchgear and controlgear 601-08

Switches other than those for SELV circuits are not allowed in zones 0, 1, or 2. This is similar to the pre-2001 requirement that every switch or other means of electrical control or adjustment shall be so situated to be normally inaccessible to a person using a fixed bath or shower. This prohibition on switches does not apply to switches and controls incorporated into fixed equipment suitable for use in the zones or to the insulating pull-cord of cord operated switches. This would mean that switches are allowed on showers and fans if the IP rating of the equipment including that of the switch is appropriate for use in the particular zone. 601-08-01

The requirements for switchgear, controlgear and accessories in locations containing a bath or shower are summarised in Table 1B.

Socket-outlets

Other than shaver socket-outlets complying with BS EN 60742 Chap 2 Sect 1 or BS EN 61558-2-5 and 12 volt SELV socket-outlets, socket-outlets are not allowed in bathrooms or shower rooms, whatever the size of the room. However, they are allowed in other locations containing a shower cubicle provided the sockets are installed outside zones 0, 1, 2 or 3 and provided the socket is protected by a RCD with a rated residual operating current $I_{\Delta n}$ not exceeding 30 mA. 601-08-01
601-08-02

In zone 3 there shall be no provision for connecting portable equipment other than the shaver and SELV socket-outlets described above. 601-08-01(ii)

Telephones

Telephones and their sockets should be installed outside zones 0, 1 and 2.

1.7 Fixed current-using equipment 601-09

Fixed current-using equipment may be installed in zones 1, 2, 3 and outside the zones but there are specific requirements for degrees of protection and it may be necessary to protect the circuit with an RCD (see Table 1B for summary of the requirements). Equipment having a rated voltage of 230 V may be installed in the above zones provided it has the appropriate IP rating and is suitable for use in the zone. This includes equipment suitable for use in the zone incorporating switches and controls. 601-05-01

1.8 Other equipment 601-09

All current-using equipment, other than portable equipment, is allowed in zone 3 and outside the zones. If installed in zone 3 it is required to be protected by an RCD with rated residual operating current $I_{\Delta n}$ not exceeding 30 mA, except for fixed current-using equipment. 601-09-03

Current-using equipment is equipment that consumes current rather than simply transmits it or switches it. Examples include appliances, luminaires, fans and heaters.

1.9 Home laundry equipment

The Regulations allow home laundry equipment such as washing machines and tumble dryers to be installed in zone 3. However, they would have to have the plug removed and be supplied by either a fused switched flex outlet complying with BS 3676 or a fused switched cord outlet connection unit complying with BS 1363-4 (also in zone 3) and be protected by a 30 mA RCD, because although heavy and perhaps plumbed in, they are not fixed equipment as such.

Chapter 2
SWIMMING POOLS AND FOUNTAINS
Sect 602

2.1 Scope

602-01

The requirements of Section 602 apply to the basins of swimming pools and paddling pools and their surrounding zones.

Except for areas especially designated as swimming pools, BS 7671 and this guidance does not apply to natural waters, such as lakes and coastal locations.

Special precautions may be necessary for swimming pools for medical purposes.

The basins of fountains, unless they are not intended to be occupied by persons and cannot be accessed without the use of ladders or similar means, are considered to be swimming pools and the requirements for all the zones of a swimming pool apply. For fountains that are not intended to be occupied, guidance is given in this chapter based upon the draft CENELEC Standard pr HD 384.7.702 S2:2001, see 2.8.

Swimming pools within the scope of an equipment standard are outside the scope of BS 7671.

For private garden ponds and private garden fountains see Chapter 16.

2.2 The risks

The risk of electric shock is increased in swimming pools and their surrounding zones by the reduction in body resistance and by good contact with earth arising from wet unclothed bodies. Equipment installed close to swimming pools and fountains is required to have appropriate degrees of protection against ingress of water.

2.3 The zones

The zones applicable to swimming pools may also be applied to the basins of fountains - see Figure 2.1. The zone is either limited by the dimensions given in Section 602 or by walls, or fixed partitions. However, the zone will extend through doorways - see Figure 2.2, unless secured to prevent unauthorised access.

602-02

All the zones extend only 2.5 metres vertically above floor level or vertically above any public access area, such as diving boards. Above the zones, any fittings suitable for the environment may be installed. The designer must bear in mind the need for access for maintenance of electrical equipment installed over the water of a swimming pool.

341-01

Fig 2.1 Example of determination of the zones of a fountain

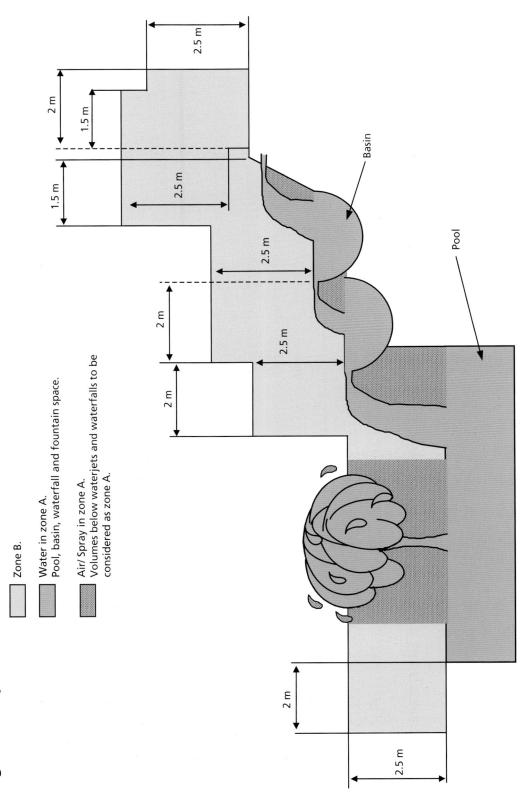

Zone B.

Water in zone A.
Pool, basin, waterfall and fountain space.

Air/ Spray in zone A.
Volumes below waterjets and waterfalls to be considered as zone A.

2.5 m

2 m

1.5 m

1.5 m

2.5 m

2.5 m

2 m

2 m

2.5 m

2.5 m

2 m

2.5 m

Basin

Pool

Fig 2.2 Examples of zone dimensions (plan) with fixed partitions of height at least 2.5 m

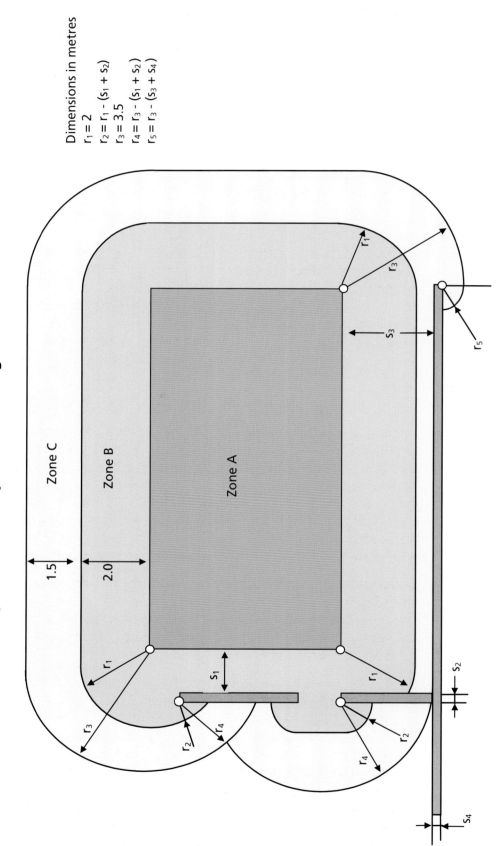

Dimensions in metres

$r_1 = 2$
$r_2 = r_1 - (s_1 + s_2)$
$r_3 = 3.5$
$r_4 = r_3 - (s_1 + s_2)$
$r_5 = r_3 - (s_3 + s_4)$

Zone C

Zone B

Zone A

1.5

2.0

2.4 Protection for safety

Local supplementary equipotential bonding is required between all extraneous-conductive-parts and the protective conductors of all exposed-conductive-parts in zones A, B and C, irrespective as to whether they are simultaneously accessible.

602-03-02

Where there are no exposed-conductive-parts, supplementary bonding is not required.

There is no particular requirement to install a metal grid in solid floors, although it is an option when installing electric floor warming. A welded grid with 200 mm window would be suitable. Where there is a metal grid, it must be connected to the local supplementary bonding.

602-03-02
602-08-04
GN5

Good permanent contact should be maintained between adjoining meshes. This usually can be achieved by binding them with metal wire for 50 mm at 1 metre intervals. Adequate quality control must be maintained and tests be carried out during installation. The joints may be required to be welded to ensure good conductivity throughout the life of the installation. Two reliable earth connections should be made to the grid, protected against corrosion and preferably at opposite ends. These should be accessible with a detachable link or other means of disconnection to facilitate testing and be suitably labelled.

602-03-02

2.5 Luminaires

It is not usually practicable to provide general illumination in a swimming pool by means of SELV luminaires, which are the only luminaires allowed in zones A and B, in which case the solution is to install ordinary luminaires at a height greater than 2.5 m above the floor/access level. Luminaires within zones A and B might be for decorative effect or to illuminate signs. Luminaires installed in the water (zone A) must be SELV with a maximum a.c. voltage of 12 V, and comply with IEC 60598-2-18 that is, IPX8 for luminaires in contact with water and IP54 for parts of luminaires not in contact with water.

602-04-01

602-08-02

Underwater lighting fitted behind watertight portholes, and serviced from behind, shall comply with the appropriate part of IEC 60598-1. They must be installed in such a way that there is no conductive connection between exposed-conductive-parts of the luminaires and conductive parts of the portholes.

In zone C, luminaires are required to be protected either by electrical separation, SELV or a 30 mA RCD. Luminaires can be protected by 30 mA RCDs but the high protective conductor currents often found in such equipment must be carefully considered. The luminaire manufacturer's advice should be sought with the objective of determining the standing protective conductor current and the maximum protective conductor current during starting so that the luminaire does not cause unwanted tripping of the 30 mA RCD. If RCD protection is used, perhaps because it is not possible to mount the luminaires more than 2.5 metres above floor level, then they should be on more than one circuit with separate RCDs. The preferred solution is use of electrical separation supplying Class II luminaires

602-08-03

supplied via insulated wire systems, since this would minimise the risk of dangerous touch voltages appearing within the installation. When refurbishing older smaller installations, there may be insufficient headroom to install the luminaires outside zone B and it may not be practicable to illuminate an area with 12 volt SELV luminaires. In situations where increasing the headroom to 2.5 m is not possible, the lighting installation must be carefully designed to allow maximum headroom and minimise accidental contact, as well as providing access for safe maintenance. Class II, 230 volt luminaires with a suitable IP rating may be used, with suitable wiring to provide a Class II installation. If it is a Class II installation, it must be under effective supervision to prevent the replacement of Class II luminaires by Class I. Additional protection by the use of RCDs should be considered, but there should be at least two lighting circuits separately protected by RCDs.

602-04-01
602-08-03

The refurbishing arrangements in the paragraph above cannot be described as complying with BS 7671. They are offered to designers as a means of dealing with an otherwise intractable problem.

120-01-03

2.6 Socket-outlets

BS 7671 recognises that it is necessary to have suitable socket-outlets in a swimming pool complex for appliances for cleaning purposes to be used only when the pool is not being used. They are generally required to be outside zones A and B. However, they are allowed within zone B when the swimming pool arrangements are such that the socket cannot be installed outside zones A and B. If the socket-outlet is installed in zone B, there are particular requirements including that it be an industrial type socket to BS EN 60309-2 and that it be protected either by an RCD or electrical separation as well as being located more than 1.25 m from zone A and at least 0.3 m above finished floor level.

602-07-01

The socket-outlets and control devices for such equipment to be used only when the pool is unoccupied should have a notice to warn the user only to use the socket when the pool is unoccupied.

All sockets in the swimming pool environs including in zones B and C are required to be industrial type to BS EN 60309-2.

602-08-01

2.7 Fire alarms and public address systems

Electrical equipment for safety systems such as fire alarms and public address are likely to be required within the pool area. This equipment should be accessible for maintenance and preferably placed outside zones A and B. Where it is not possible to locate equipment outside zone B, it should be more than 1.25 metres outside zone A and as high above floor level as is practicable, in order to keep the equipment dry. The equipment will need to be of an insulated construction and have IP coding as required in Regulation 602-05-01. Local microphones must be SELV or connected via isolating transformers, and telephones, if required, should be cordless type within the zones with a base unit installed outside the zones.

602-05-01

2.8 Fountains

General

The basins of fountains and their surroundings, unless persons are prevented from gaining access to them without the use of ladders or similar means, are treated as swimming pools.

The rules for basins of fountains to which access is prevented are amended as follows :

In zones A and B one of the following protective measures shall be used:

- SELV, the source for SELV being installed outside zones A and B
- earthed equipotential bonding and automatic disconnection of supply using an RCD with a rated residual operating current not exceeding 30 mA
- electrical separation, the separation source supplying only one item of equipment and installed outside zones A and B.

In zone C of fountains there are no requirements additional to the general rules.

Electrical equipment of fountains

Electrical equipment in zones A and B must be made inaccessible e.g. by the use of mesh, or grids. Luminaires in zones A and B are required to be fixed and should comply with BS EN 60598-2-18, Luminaires for swimming pools and similar locations.

Electric pumps should comply with BS EN 60335-2-41.

Additional requirements for the wiring of fountains

Cables supplying equipment in zone A should be installed outside the basin i.e. in zone B where possible, and run to the equipment in the basin by the shortest practical route.

Cables supplying equipment in zone A shall have been declared by the supplier to be suitable for continuous immersion in water.

Chapter 3
HOT AIR SAUNAS

Sect 603

3.1 Scope

The requirements of BS 7671 for saunas apply only to those where the sauna equipment complies with BS EN 60335-2-53 : 1997 - Electric sauna heating appliances. BS EN 60335 specifies requirements for appliances having a rated input not exceeding 20 kW.

603-01-01

3.2 The risks

There are two particular aspects of saunas that make them special locations :

1. increased risk of electric shock because of extremely high humidity, lack of clothing, reduced skin resistance and large contact areas

2. very high temperatures in certain zones.

3.3 Shock protection

Protection against electric shock is provided by not allowing any electrical equipment that is not part of the heating appliance or strictly necessary for the operation of the sauna such as, sauna thermostat, sauna cut-out and luminaires. Light switches must be placed outside the cabin and socket-outlets are not allowed within the cabin. It is advisable not to install sockets near the cabin, the same criteria as for swimming pools should be adopted.

603-08

A sauna is often part of a health or fitness suite and may be associated with a swimming pool, showers or bathing facilities. Such premises should be considered as a whole, and it must be borne in mind that the sauna cabin may well be located within the zones of the swimming pool.

603-01-01

The requirements for protection against direct and indirect contact in saunas are similar to those for bathrooms and swimming pools.

The wiring

All wiring should be carried out in flexible cables or cords, having 180 °C rubber insulation, complying with BS 7919 : 2001, and using insulated wiring enclosures complying with general Class II requirements.

603-07-01
Table 4H3A

The zones

The zones are temperature zones, dimensioned down from the ceiling, up from the floor and around the sauna. This allows application of the zones whatever the size of the sauna cabin.

Heating elements

The heating elements incorporated in a sauna are likely to be metal sheathed. These, unless specified as having waterproof seals, may absorb moisture and cause the operation of a 30 mA RCD, if installed. There is no particular requirement in Section 603 to protect the sauna heater circuit with an RCD. If it is wished to install a 30 mA RCD, it is wise to check its suitability with the heating equipment manufacturer and that the elements installed are suitable for protection by a 30 mA device. An RCD having a lower sensitivity e.g. 100 mA will have a greater resistance to unwanted tripping caused by the high protective conductor current of the heating elements.

Chapter 4
CONSTRUCTION SITE INSTALLATIONS
Sect 604

4.1   Scope

604-01

Section 604 applies to all sites of construction work including the repair or alteration of existing buildings and demolition work.   604-01-01

Any installation where the general requirements of the Regulations are to be met with respect to the permanency of the works and with respect to freedom from environmental and mechanical risks associated with construction, is outside the scope of this section of BS 7671.   110-01-01

A construction site electrical installation is considered to be movable as this is the nature of much of the equipment. The installation will normally include step-down, earthed centre tap, transformers supplying reduced low voltage hand tools such as lamps, drills etc.

BS 7375 : 1996 Code of Practice for distribution of electricity on construction and building sites is the relevant Standard.

4.2   The risks

Construction sites are potentially dangerous in many ways, but only those dangers that are associated with the risks of electric shock or burns are considered here. The risk of electric shock is high on a construction site because :

1.   of the possibility of damage to cables and equipment

2.   of the wide use of hand tools with trailing leads

3.   of the accessibility of many extraneous-conductive-parts, which cannot practically be bonded

4.   the works are generally open to the elements.

4.3   Supplies

BS 7671, whilst restricting IT supplies, allows TN or TT supplies to be made available to construction sites, and the Electricity Safety, Quality and Continuity Regulations 2002 allow TN or TT supplies. However, distribution network operators may be reluctant to provide a protective multiple earthed (PME) supply. Because of the considerable amount of extraneous-conductive-parts generally accessible there is difficulty in installing and maintaining the equipotential bonding required by BS 7671. As there is no specific prohibition on the use of a PME supply in BS 7671 and it is to be presumed that if it could be demonstrated to the distributor that the PME earth would only be used   604-03-01 for site huts etc., and a TT installation used for the construction site proper, then a PME earth may well be made available. However, this approach is not generally recommended and applies only in exceptional circumstances, such as very large sites. If it is adopted, suitable warnings should be posted at TN supply points and TN distribution boards, that supplies from this board are not to be made available to the construction site proper.

4.4   Reduced low voltage

604-02-02 (iii)   BS 7671 requires the use of reduced low voltage supplies for all portable equipment, small mobile plant and local lighting up to 2 kW. 110 V reduced low voltage supplies with the centre point of the secondary winding of the step-down transformer earthed, limit the voltage to earth to 55 volts for single-phase supplies and 63.5 volts to earth for three-phase equipment (See Figure 4.1).

The movable reduced low voltage 110 volt installation equipment is required to comply with BS 4363 and BS EN 60439-4. 110 V plugs and sockets to BS EN 60309-2 (or BS 4343) are coloured yellow. It is usual practice for all cables in the movable installation to also have yellow sheaths, so that the safety system can be identified, however this is not a requirement of BS 7671 or the British Standard for Building Site Installations, BS 7375.

604-09-01
604-12-02

Limiting the voltage to 55 or 63.5 volts between a live conductor and earth effectively eliminates the risk of dangerous electric shock to exposed-conductive-parts.

Fig 4.1 Reduced low voltage supplies

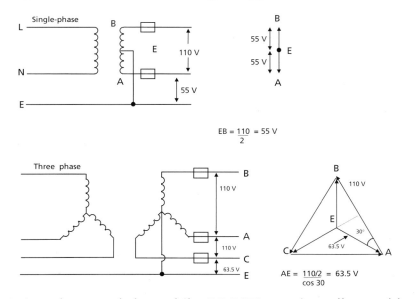

It is to be noted that whilst BS 7671 requires all portable equipment etc. on building sites to be supplied from a reduced low voltage supply or SELV, the Health and Safety Executive have advised that the use of 230 volt hand tools protected by an individual 30 milliamp RCD may be acceptable (See HSE Guidance Note HS(G)141 Electrical Safety on Construction Sites).

BS 7671 allows standard BS 1363 socket-outlets on building sites if protected by 30 mA RCDs. However, BS 7671 requires portable hand-held tools, portable hand lamps, local lighting up to 2 kW and small mobile plant up to 3.75 kW to be supplied from a reduced low voltage 110 V, 1-phase, centre point earthed system or a 110 V, 3-phase, star point earthed system.

604-08-03

604-02-02

Fixed equipment can be supplied at 230 V, and fixed equipment rated at over 3.75 kW (e.g. cranes) at 400 V three-phase. The notes of guidance to the Electricity Safety, Quality and Continuity Regulations advise that special consideration be given to the earthing and protection arrangements; see guidance on additional earth electrodes for PME supplies in paragraph 9.3 of Guidance Note 5.

GN5
Protection against Electric Shock

4.5   Maximum earth fault loop impedances

604-04

BS 7671 specifies reduced disconnection times for TN systems and provides maximum earth fault loop impedance tables for devices so that the reduced disconnection times are met. It is to be noted that these disconnection times apply for nominal voltages to earth of 120 volts and above (Table 604A) and for 230 volts (Tables 604B1, 604B2). This means that the reduced times do not apply to 110 volt centre-tapped systems, for which a maximum 5 second disconnection time is allowed. If reduced times were applied, the length of cables would be so limited as to make the use of the reduced low voltage system impracticable. Experience over some 50 to 60 years has not revealed any problems in this respect.

604-04-03
604-04-04

604-04-06

The loop impedance at the end of a circuit fed from the secondary of a step-down transformer Z_{sec} is given by :

$$Z_{sec} = Z_p \times \left(\frac{V_s}{V_p}\right)^2 + \frac{Z\%tran}{100} \frac{(V_s)^2}{VA} + (R_1 + R_2)_s$$

where :

Z_p = loop impedance of the primary circuit including that of the source supply.

$Z\%tran$ = percentage impedance of the step-down transformer.

VA = rating of the step-down transformer.

V_s = secondary voltage.

V_p = primary voltage.

$(R_1 + R_2)_s$ = phase and protective conductor resistances of the secondary circuit.

If data on the step-down transformer is not available, this may be simplified to:

$$Z_{sec} = 1.25\left\{ Z_p \times \left(\frac{V_s}{V_p}\right)^2 + (R_1 + R_2)_s \right\}$$

$$Z_{sec} = 1.25\left\{ (Z_e + 2R_1)_p \times \left(\frac{V_s}{V_p}\right)^2 + (R_1 + R_2)_s \right\}$$

where :

1.25 is a factor to compensate for an underestimate.

Z_e = the external phase-neutral/earth loop impedance.

$(2R_1)_p$ = the primary circuit phase plus neutral conductor impedance.

RCDs are commonly used to protect building sites, the installation being treated as a TT system with a separate earth electrode. See paragraph 5.5 of the chapter on agricultural installations for maximum values of the resistance to earth (R_A). 604-05-01

4.6   Isolation and switching

604-11   Section 604 repeats emergency switching requirements of Section 463 that emergency switching shall be provided on the supply to all the equipment from which it may be necessary to disconnect **all live** conductors in order **to remove a hazard**. 604-11-03
463-01-01

The requirement is to provide emergency switching where there is a need to remove a hazard, and the switching requirement is for disconnection of all live conductors, that is including the neutral.

Every circuit supplying equipment shall be fed from a distribution assembly complying with BS EN 60439-4 and BS 4363. 604-09-01

4.7   Protection against the weather and dust

All equipment that is part of the movable installation is required to have a degree of protection appropriate to the external influence. Equipment for external use must be at least IP44. However equipment installed in a weather protected location such as an office being refurbished, would have no specific IP requirement.

4.8   Inspection and testing

Fixed installation

It is recommended that the maximum period between inspections of construction site installations is 3 months. GN3
Inspection &
Testing

Fixed installation RCDs should additionally be tested daily (using the integral test button). Should RCDs be used to protect portable equipment they must be tested by the operative before each period of use (using the integral test button) and by the responsible person every 3 months (using an RCD tester).

Movable equipment

Recommended intervals for Inspection and testing are given by Table 4A below:

TABLE 4A FREQUENCY OF INSPECTION AND TESTING OF EQUIPMENT

Type of Premises	Type of Equipment (Note 1)	User Checks (Note 2)	Class I		Class II (Note 4)	
			Formal Visual Inspection (Note 3)	Combined Inspection and Testing (Note 5)	Formal Visual Inspection (Note 3)	Combined Inspection and Testing (Note 5)
Construction sites	S	None	1 month	3 months	1 month	3 months
	IT	None	1 month	3 months	1 month	3 months
110 V }	M (Note 6)	weekly	1 month	3 months	1 month	3 months
equipment }	P (Note 6)	weekly	1 month	3 months	1 month	3 months
}	H (Note 6)	weekly	1 month	3 months	1 month	3 months

Notes :

(1) S   Stationary equipment
IT   Information technology equipment
M   Movable equipment
P   Portable equipment
H   Hand-held equipment

(2)   User checks are not recorded unless a fault is found.

(3)   The formal visual inspection may form part of the combined inspection and tests when they coincide, and must be recorded.

(4)   If class of equipment is not known, it must be tested as Class I.

(5)   The results of combined inspections and test are recorded.

(6)   110 V earthed centre-tapped supply. 230 V portable or hand-held equipment must be supplied via a 30 mA RCD and should be tested before each period of use.

Chapter 5
AGRICULTURAL AND HORTICULTURAL PREMISES

Sect 605

5.1 Scope

605-01   Section 605 provides particular requirements for farms, greenhouses and general horticultural and agricultural premises. Particular reference is made to locations where livestock is kept such as stables, chicken-houses, piggeries. The use of the expression 'livestock' would imply that the animals are kept for commercial purposes and the requirements would not apply in domestic premises where there might be cats and dogs, but are appropriate where there is a stable.

605-01-01

Some of the particular requirements are not easily applicable to larger agricultural premises such as packing stations, grain stores and cold stores, particularly the requirement for the installation of a 500 mA RCD to protect against fire. In such circumstances, the general intent of the Regulations must be considered, which is that they apply to farms and the like. Guidance is given in paragraph 5.6. Protection needs to be provided as appropriate.

Houses, shops and offices associated with farms are not required to meet the special requirements for agricultural and horticultural premises.

5.2 The risks

The particular risks associated with farms and horticultural premises are:

1. general accessibility of extraneous-conductive-parts and impracticality of supplementary or main bonding such extraneous parts

2. an onerous environment with respect to mechanical damage, exposure to the weather, corrosive effects (from water, animal urine, farm chemicals etc.)

3. a mechanically hazardous area due to electromechanical equipment, mills and mixers, and mechanical drives of all kinds

4. rodent damage to (gnawing of) cables, leading to fire risks

5. storage of flammable materials e.g. straw and grain.

5.3   Electricity supplies

Because of the practical difficulties in bonding all accessible extraneous-conductive-parts electricity distribution companies might not provide a PME earth to agricultural and horticultural installations.

The DTI Guidance on the Electricity Safety, Quality and Continuity Regulations 2002 advise {9(4)} that special consideration should be given to the earthing and bonding requirements to farms where it may prove difficult to attach and maintain all the necessary equipotential bonding connections for a PME supply.

A TN-S supply is unlikely to be provided by a distributor as a routine unless the installation is particularly large and early application is made. Alternatively, consideration should be given to installing an additional earth electrode, see paragraph 9.3 ofGuidance Note 5. It is most likely that the installation will be required to be TT. Farm installations are relatively large and there can be unwanted tripping of an RCD where there is equipment having a high protective conductor current and/or where several items of such equipment are protected by a high sensitivity RCD. Attention is drawn to Regulation 605-10-01 and the requirement to install an RCD having a rated residual operating current not exceeding 500 mA to provide protection against fire caused by protective conductor currents. An RCD having a 300 mA sensitivity is likely to be the most appropriate to install at the origin of farm installations.

GN5 Protection against Electric Shock

605-10-01

The choice of sensitivity of the main RCD is also influenced by the nature of processed or stored material. Locations with a risk of fire due to the nature of processed or stored materials should be protected against the effects of insulation faults by a 300 mA RCD.

482-02-06

There is a need to provide discrimination between 30 mA RCDs, RCBOs or SRCDs required for socket-outlets and the main RCD. Such discrimination is assured when the main RCD has a rated residual tripping current of 100 mA or greater and incorporates an intentional time delay.

Alternatively, the RCDs may be separated as shown in Figure 5.2.

Fig 5.1 RCDs in series

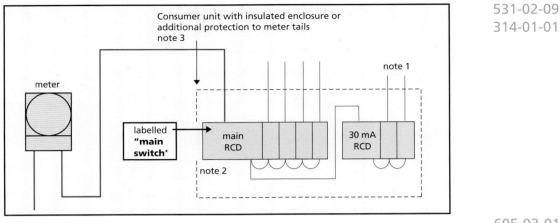

531-02-09
314-01-01

Note 1   socket-outlet circuits

Note 2   if the RCD is also the isolating switch it must be clearly labelled.

Note 3   the risk of faults to exposed-conductive-parts on the supply side of the RCD must be minimised as such faults are not detected by the RCD

605-03-01
514-01-01
537-02-09
531-04-01

Fig 5.2 Separate RCDs

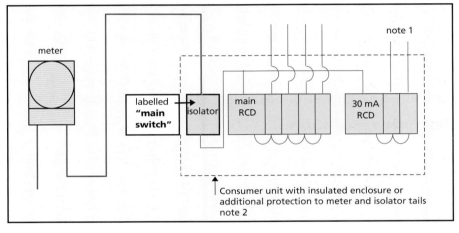

Note 1   socket-outlet circuits

Note 2   the risk of faults to exposed-conductive-parts on the supply side of the RCD must be minimised as such faults are not detected by the RCD

605-03-01
531-04-01

It is to be noted that in TT installations isolators are required to switch all live conductors including the neutral.

460-01-04

5.4   Protection against electric shock

Where a TN installation can be adopted, the disconnection time for 230 volt installations is required to be reduced from 0.4 s to 0.2 s. This reduced disconnection time applies to locations in which livestock is intended to be kept and does not apply generally.

605-05-01
605-05-02

IEC Report 479-3 "Effects of current passing through the body of livestock" provides some guidance on the susceptibility of farm animals to shock. The hide of an animal is particularly resistant to shock having an impedance when dry of 1000 ohms, however, animals do have four feet in contact with the ground and this reduces the body impedance to earth. A particularly susceptible area is a wet nose. However, the report states that on balance for the protection of animals, the same precautions as for people are generally appropriate.

IEC 479-3

However, animals will detect relatively small voltage gradients between front and rear legs, and between conductive part potentials and earth.

This can result in, for example, a marked reluctance for cows to enter milking parlours because of potential differences. These potential differences can arise from a number of causes. If the electricity supply is PME, at the end of a long run there is likely to be a potential between the PME earth and true earth. In such situations there will need to be supplementary bonding. The connection of an earth electrode to the main earthing terminal will also reduce touch voltages. The necessary resistance to earth will depend on the load and need be not less than say 20 ohms, see 9.3 of Guidance Note 5. Alternatively the installation should be disconnected from the PME earth and treated as TT.

GN5
Protection
Against
Electric Shock

It is well known that animals have received shocks that are associated with electrical installations. It is likely that lightning strikes on overhead lines conducted to earth via earth electrodes at the bottom of a pole produce voltage gradients that are fatal to animals because of the wide spacing of their feet. If there is concern in this respect the location of earth electrodes should be discussed with the electricity distribution company.

All circuits supplying socket-outlets (other than any from a SELV supply) are required to be protected by a 30 mA RCD.

605-03-01

5.5 Earth electrode resistances

Where protection against electric shock is provided by an RCD the following condition is required to be fulfilled :

605-06-01

$R_A I_{\Delta n} \leq 25$ volts

where :

R_A is the sum of the resistances of the earth electrode and the protective conductor(s) connecting it to the exposed-conductive-parts

$I_{\Delta n}$ is the rated residual operating current of the RCD.

The resistance of the protective conductors is negligible compared with the resistance to earth of the electrode. Therefore R_A approximates to the resistance of the earth electrode to earth and must be less than the figures given below :

Rated residual operating current $I_{\Delta n}$ mA	Earth electrode resistance R_A Ω
30	833
100	250
300	83
500	50

In practice, R_A should never be greater than 200 ohms otherwise it may prove unstable.

5.6   Protection against fire

RCDs of a rated residual operating current not exceeding 500 mA are required to provide protection against fire - see Figures 5.1 and 5.2. These must protect all equipment except that essential for the welfare of livestock, for example poultry ventilation fans, see Figure 5.3.   605-10-01

An RCD having a 300 mA sensitivity is likely to be the most sensitive general type RCD appropriate to install in all but the largest installations, where the high protective conductor current resulting from the large number of pieces of equipment or inrush currents can cause unwanted tripping of the RCD. Where problems are anticipated, for example in a large grain handling installation or on farm premises with preparation and processing facilities, decisions will need to be made by the designer as to whether the installation can be subdivided or 500 mA RCD protection omitted from all or part of the installation - see Figure 5.3.

Rodent damage is a major cause of farm fires and this must be taken into account by the designer and installer. Cables should be installed and routed with such potential damage in mind. For example, in a livestock building cables should be routed on the underside of the ceiling rather than in a false roof. Steel conduit provides a good degree of protection.

5.7   External influences

Electrical equipment installed as in normal use , that is unless specially protected from the local environment, shall be at least IP44.   605-11-01

IPX4 provides protection against water splashing

IPX5 provides protection against water jets from any direction

IPX6 provides protection against powerful water jets from any direction

See Appendix B of Guidance Note 1 for details of the IP code and the drip proof symbols.

Fig 5.3 Large TN farm installation schematic drawing with essential supplies

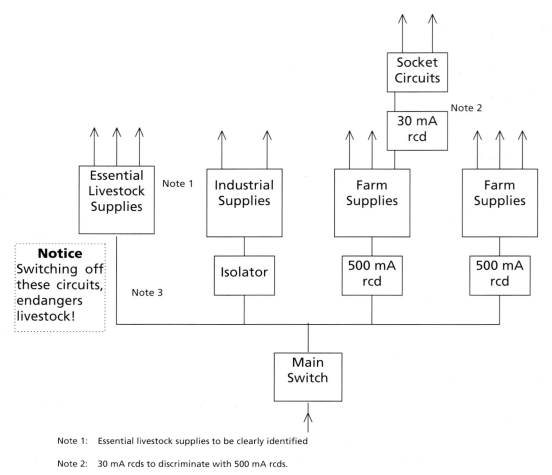

Note 1:   Essential livestock supplies to be clearly identified

Note 2:   30 mA rcds to discriminate with 500 mA rcds.

Note 3:   Isolator omitted to prevent inadvertent operation,

Chapter 6
RESTRICTIVE CONDUCTIVE LOCATIONS
Sect 606

6.1 Scope

A restrictive conductive location is constructed mainly of metallic or 606-01 conductive parts and within it movement is restricted. It is likely that a person in a restrictive conductive location will be in good contact with conductive surroundings and escape will be restricted in the event of an electric shock.

The particular requirements of Section 606 do not apply to locations which allow persons freedom of bodily movement, that is, to enter, work and leave the location without physical constraint. The type of locations that are being considered includes boiler shells, cable gantries, small tunnels, metal sewers etc.

6.2 The risks

In many ordinary locations in the event of direct or indirect contact there is usually limited access to earthed metal. As a result the likelihood of receiving a shock current of sufficient magnitude to have harmful physiological effects is low. This is not so with a restrictive conductive location.

In a restrictive conductive location there is little opportunity to move away from the shock. Contact resistance is low due to high contact areas and perspiration, so that body currents are high and the risk of ventricular fibrillation is high - see Figure 7.1 in Chapter 7. There are other effects of electric shock that are also relevant in such locations. Muscles used to breath can be constrained by body currents and shocks to the head can paralyse the breathing function.

6.3 The particular requirements

For protection against direct contact the use of obstacles and placing out of reach are not permitted in restrictive conductive locations. Protection against indirect contact should be by one of the following 606-04-01 methods:

1) SELV with insulation and/or barriers,

2) automatic disconnection of supply augmented by supplementary bonding,

3) electrical separation with only one item of equipment connected to each secondary winding,

4) the use of Class II equipment further protected by a 30 mA RCD.

These are in no particular order of priority.

Hand lamps and hand tools are required to have a SELV supply or, in the case of hand tools, be protected by electrical separation. The safety source is required to be installed outside the location unless it is permanently fixed as part of the fixed installation.

606-04-02
606-04-04
606-04-06

Chapter 7
EARTHING REQUIREMENTS FOR THE INSTALLATION OF EQUIPMENT HAVING HIGH PROTECTIVE CONDUCTOR CURRENTS

Sect 607

7.1 Scope

607-01   The requirements of this section apply to :   607-01-01

1)   equipment between the final circuit wiring and current-using equipment where the protective conductor current exceeds 3.5 mA

2)   final circuits where the accumulated protective conductor current is expected to exceed 10 mA.

The use of information technology equipment, which has low electrical loading but relatively high protective conductor currents, often requires special precautions to be taken. A final circuit can accept many items of IT equipment and remain within the rating of the circuit, but the protective conductor currents resulting may be relatively very high.

Modern luminaires may also draw sufficient protective conductor current to require the precautions of Section 607 to be taken.

7.2 The risks

The risk associated with final circuits with high protective conductor currents is that resulting from discontinuity of the protective conductor. In installations where there are high protective conductor currents, serious shocks can be received from accessible conductive parts connected to protective conductors which are not connected to the main earthing terminal. This shock risk is extended to all the items of equipment on the particular circuit, whether they individually have high protective conductor currents or not. The more equipment that is connected to a circuit, the wider is spread the risk, and the greater is the hazard.

IEC Publication 479-1 the effects of current passing through the human body (BS PD 6519-1) advises that for body currents less than 10 mA, there are usually no harmful physiological effects.

As the body currents increase, so the risk of organic damage and probability of ventricular fibrillation increases, see Figure 7.1.

Section 607 prescribes particular requirements for installations with final circuit and distribution circuit protective conductor currents exceeding 10 mA. If equipment has a protective conductor current of

10 mA, the impedance that allows this at 230 V is 23,000 Ω. The body plus footwear impedance is usually about 2,000 Ω (in dry conditions) - see Table 1A in Chapter 1. Consequently, body impedance does not effectively limit touch current. If a person touches the exposed-conductive-parts of such equipment when the protective conductor is disconnected, the current conducted through the body is 230 / (23,000 + 2,000) that is 9.2 mA, a minimal reduction.

Fig 7.1 Time/current zones of effects of a.c. currents 15 Hz to 100 Hz

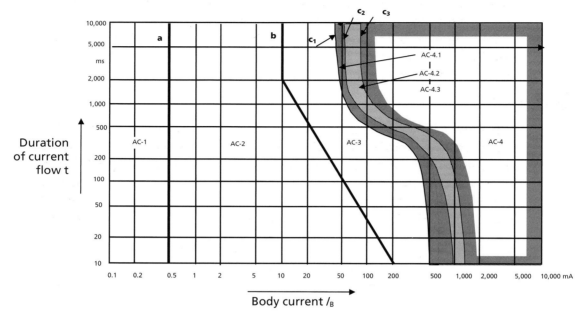

From fig 14 of IEC 479-1

NOTE - As regards ventricular fibrillation, this figure relates to the effects of current which flows in the path left hand to both feet. The threshold values for durations of current flow below 0.2 s apply only to current flowing during the vulnerable period of the cardiac cycle.

Zone designation	Zone limits	Physiological effects
AC-1	Up to 0.5 mA (line a)	Usually no reaction.
AC-2	From 0.5 mA (line a) up to line b	Usually no harmful physiological effects.
AC-3	From line b up to curve c_1	Usually no organic damage to be expected. Likelihood of cramp like muscular contractions and difficulty in breathing for durations of current flow longer than 2 s. Reversible disturbances of formation and conduction of impulses in the heart, including atrial fibrillation and transient cardiac arrest without ventricular fibrillation increasing with current magnitude and time.
AC-4	Above curve c_1	Increasing with magnitude and time, dangerous pathophysiological effects such as cardiac arrest, breathing arrest and severe burns may occur in addition to the effects of zone 3.
AC-4.1	Between c_1 and c_2	Probability of ventricular fibrillation increasing up to about 5 %.
AC-4.2	Between c_2 and c_3	Probability of ventricular fibrillation up to about 50 %.
AC-4.3	Beyond curve c_3	Probability of ventricular fibrillation above 50 %.
For durations of current flow below 10 ms, the limit for the body current for line b remains constant at a value of 200 mA.		

From table 4 of IEC 479-1 protective conductor currents exceeding 10 mA can have harmful effects and precautions need to be taken, see Figure 7.1.

The requirements of Section 607 are intended to increase the reliability of the connection of protective conductors to equipment and to earth, when the circuit protective conductor current exceeds 10 mA. This normally requires duplication of the protective conductor or an increase in its size. The increased size is not to allow for thermal effects of the protective conductor currents, which are insignificant, but to provide for greater mechanical strength and, it is intended, a more reliable connection with earth. Duplication of a protective conductor each with independent terminations, is likely to be more effective than an increase in size.

607-02-03
607-02-04
607-03-01

7.3 Equipment

Note that BS EN 60950, the standard for the safety of information technology equipment, including electrical business equipment, requires equipment with a protective conductor current exceeding 3.5 mA to have internal protective conductor cross-sectional areas not less than 1.0 mm^2 and also requires a label bearing the following or similar wording fixed adjacent to the equipment primary power connection:

> HIGH LEAKAGE CURRENT
> Earth connection essential
> before connecting the supply

or

> WARNING HIGH TOUCH CURRENTS
> Earth connection essential
> before connecting the supply

Regulation 607-02-02 requires a single item of equipment, if the protective conductor current exceeds 3.5 mA but does not exceed 10 mA, to be permanently connected or connected by a plug and socket complying with BS EN 60309-2. If the protective conductor current exceeds 10 mA the requirements of Regulations 607-02-03 and 607-02-04 for a high integrity protective earth connection must be met.

607-02-02

607-02-03
607-02-04

7.4 Socket-outlet circuits

Labelling

607-03-02

Distribution boards supplying circuits with high protective conductor currents must be labelled accordingly so that persons working on the boards can ensure they maintain the protective precautions taken.

Ring circuits

607-03-01

Ring circuits provide duplication of the protective conductor, and if the ends of the protective conductor are separately terminated at the distribution board and at the sockets, the requirements of Section 607 will be met, see Figure 7.2. Sockets are available with two earth terminals for this purpose.

607-02-05

Fig 7.2 Ring final circuit supplying socket-outlets (total protective conductor current exceeding 10 mA).

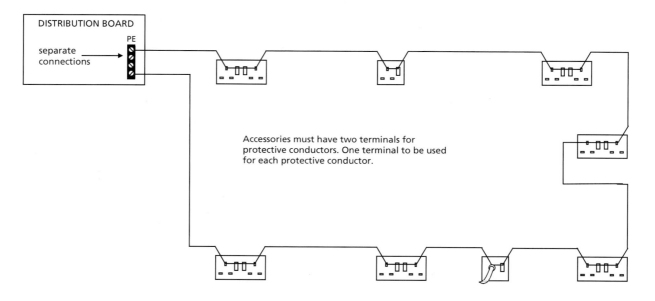

Accessories must have two terminals for protective conductors. One terminal to be used for each protective conductor.

Radial circuits

607-03-01(ii)

Radial circuits supplying sockets where the protective conductor current is expected to exceed 10 mA are required to have a high integrity protective conductor connection. This can often be most effectively provided by a separate duplicate protective conductor connecting the last socket directly back to the distribution board as shown in Figure 7.3. This will provide a duplicate connection for each socket on the circuit. The following requirements apply:

1. all socket-outlets must have two protective conductor terminal, one for each protective conductor

2. the duplicate protective conductors shall be separately connected at the distribution board.

Note: To reduce interference effects, the duplicate protective conductor should be run in close proximity to the other conductors of the circuit.

Fig 7.3 Radial circuit supplying socket-outlets (total protective conductor current exceeding 10 mA), with duplicate protective conductor.

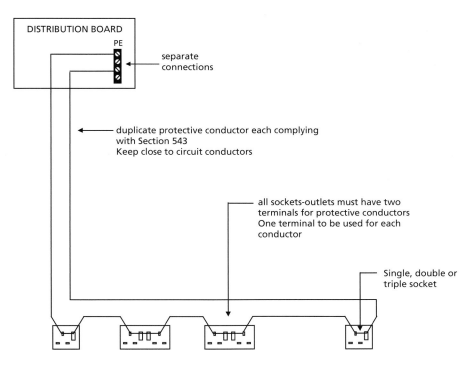

DISTRIBUTION BOARD

PE

separate connections

duplicate protective conductor each complying with Section 543
Keep close to circuit conductors

all sockets-outlets must have two terminals for protective conductors
One terminal to be used for each conductor

Single, double or triple socket

Figure 7.3 shows typical arrangement.

Busbar systems

Busbar systems are often adopted by designers for supplying IT equipment, see Figure 7.4. These may be radial 30 or 32 amp busbars with tee-offs to individual sockets. The main PE busbar will need to meet one or more of the requirements of Regulation 607-02-04, having a protective conductor with a cross-sectional area not less than 10 mm^2 or duplicate protective conductors each of cross-sectional area sufficient to meet the requirements of Section 543.

607-02-04

543-01-01

Fig 7.4 Spurs from a 30 A or 32 A busbar

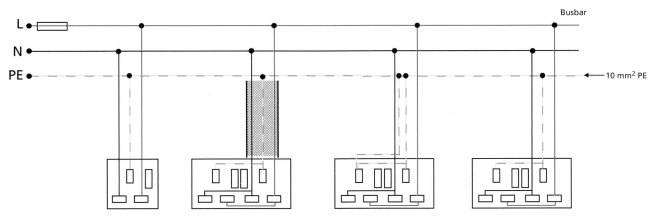

Busbar

L

N

PE

10 mm^2 PE

If protective conductor current is likely to exceed 10 mA a 4 mm^2 PE with mechanical protection or a duplicate PE is required. Otherwise one PE is sufficient

The sockets are often connected as spurs off such a busbar system. If the protective conductor current is expected to be less than 3.5 mA, there is no need for duplication of the protective conductor on the spur from the radial busbar to the socket. Where the protective conductor current is likely to exceed 10 mA then a single copper protective conductor having a cross-sectional area not less than 4 mm^2 and enclosed to provide additional mechanical can be used.

607-02-04

It is necessary for the designer to confirm that the disconnection time of the 30 or 32 amp device feeding the busbar is sufficiently fast to provide adiabatic fault protection to the spurred conductors. This almost certainly will be so for, say, 2.5 mm^2 conductors and disconnection within the 0.4 s required, but this must be confirmed. Overload protection is not required on the socket spur from the busbar provided the spur cable rating exceeds 13 A, since the outlet is a standard 13 A and only plugs fitted with a maximum 13 A fuse can be connected. Hence, overload of the conductor cannot occur, and the 30 or 32 A device can provide adequate fault protection.

434-03-03

473-01-04

7.5 Requirements for TT systems

607-05-01

For TT systems it is required that :

$$2 \times I_{pc} \times R_A \leq 50 \text{ volts}$$

where :

I_{pc} is the protective conductor current

R_A is the resistance to earth of the installation earth electrode.

This is to limit the voltage between true earth and any equipment connected to the earth electrode to 25 V.

7.6 Requirements for IT systems

Equipment having a protective conductor current exceeding 3.5 mA in normal service must not be connected directly to an IT system.

607-06-01

Chapter 8
CARAVANS, TENTS AND CARAVAN PARKS
Sect 608

8.1 Scope

Section 608 is divided into two divisions.

608-01 Division one - Electrical Installations in caravans and motor caravans

608-09 Division two - Electrical installations in caravan parks

A caravan is defined as a trailer vehicle for leisure accommodation used for touring on public roads; a motor caravan is similarly defined as a self-propelled vehicle.   Part 2

8.2 The risks

The risks specifically associated with installations in caravans and motor caravans arise from :

i) Open circuit faults of the PEN conductor of PME supplies raising the potential to true earth of all metalwork (including that of caravans if connected) to dangerous levels

ii) Incorrect polarity at the pitch supply point

iii) Inability to establish an equipotential zone external to the vehicle

iv) Possible loss of earthing due to long supply cable runs, connecting devices exposed to weather and flexible cord connections liable to mechanical damage

v) Vibration while the vehicle is moving causing faults within the caravan installation.

Particular requirements to reduce the above risks include:

i) Prohibition of the connection of exposed- and extraneous-conductive-parts of a caravan or motor caravan to a PME terminal   608-13-05

ii) Additional protection by 30 mA RCDs in both the vehicle and the park installation. Double-pole isolating switch and final circuit cbs in the caravan or motor caravan   608-03-02 608-07-04 608-04-01 608-13-05

iii) Internal wiring by flexible or stranded cables of cross-sectional area 1.5 mm^2 or greater. Additional cable supports. Segregation of low voltage and extra-low voltage circuits.   608-06-01 608-06-02 608-06-05

8.3   Legislation and standards

Regulation 9(4) of the Electricity Safety, Quality and Continuity Regulations 2002 prohibits the connection of the supply neutral of a PME supply to any metalwork in a caravan or boat.

Caravan parks (sites) in the United Kingdom are subject to the provisions of the Caravans Control of Development Act 1960. This empowers local authorities to issue licences and to impose conditions, generally in accordance with model standards for residential parks (revised 1977) and for touring parks (issued 1983). The Model Standards call up the requirements of BS 7671 for the electrical installation in the caravan park.

The 1960 Act also empowers certain "exempted bodies" such as the Caravan Club and the Camping and Caravanning Club to issue certificates in respect of parks for use by their own members.

While there is no legislation specific to electrical installations in caravans, BS 4626 Touring trailer caravans indicates that any electrical installation at mains voltage shall comply with BS 7671.

8.4   Division one, Caravans and motor caravans

8.4.1 Introduction

It is to be noted that Division one of Section 608 specifically applies to caravans (defined in Part 2 as touring trailer caravans) and motor caravans, i.e. vehicles intended to be moved frequently from point to point. Leisure accommodation that is not intended for frequent movement, for example mobile homes, are not covered by Division one but may nevertheless be subject to the prohibition by the Electricity Safety, Quality and Continuity Regulations 2002 on connection of caravan metalwork to the neutral conductor of a PME supply.

608-01-01

8.4.2 Equipotential bonding

The minimum cross-sectional area required for bonding conductors to extraneous-conductive-parts of caravans is 4 mm^2 irrespective of the provision of protection against mechanical damage. Metal sheets forming part of the structure of the caravan or motor caravan need not be bonded; also, when a caravan is made substantially of insulating material, metal parts that are unlikely to become live in the event of a fault are similarly exempt from bonding.

608-03-04

8.4.3 Provision of RCDs

For protection against indirect contact, only two methods are acceptable for caravan installations, namely, automatic disconnection of supply and/or Class II equipment. As it is not possible to ensure that only Class II equipment will be used, a double-pole RCD, which may also serve as the main isolating switch, must be provided within the caravan. This is additional to the RCD required at the pitch socket-outlet and affords protection within the caravan. The RCD at the pitch socket provides protection against faults between the pitch socket and the caravan and also in the caravan.

608-03-01

608-03-02

608-13-05

8.4.4 Protection against overcurrent

Overcurrent protective devices for final circuits are required to disconnect both phase and neutral conductors, necessitating the use of double-pole circuit-breakers.

8.4.5 Selection and erection of equipment

More than one electrically independent installation is allowed, provided the separation and segregation requirements of Regulation 528-01-02 are met. This allows for the usual battery-fed 12 V circuits for interior lighting in accordance with BS EN 1648: Leisure accommodation vehicles 12 V direct current extra-low voltage installations and for the road lighting circuits in accordance with the Road Vehicle Lighting Regulations 1989. The independent circuits must be compartmentalised or insulated for the highest voltage present, that is 230 V.

608-05-01

528-01-02

8.4.6 Switchgear and controlgear

The inlet to the caravan is required to be two-pole and earthing contact and to comply with BS EN 60309-2 with the earthing contact at key position 6 h; it is normally rated at 16 A and coloured blue. Similar inlets of higher current rating, e.g. 32 A, may be provided where required.

608-07-01

The inlet is to be installed in an enclosure and connected directly to the main isolating switch; this connection should be as short as practicable and should be protected against mechanical damage because it is not isolated by the double-pole main switch. A notice should be fixed near the inlet advising the voltage, frequency and current rating of the caravan installation.

608-07-02

608-07-03

The main isolating switch must switch the phase and the neutral conductors and be "suitably placed for ready operation" within the caravan.

608-07-04

8.4.7 The connecting flexible cable

This should be a flex 25 ±2 metres long to harmonized code designation H07RN-F or H05VV-F and not less than 2.5 mm^2 if the plug is 16 A or 4 mm^2 if it is 32 A. A BS EN 60309-2 plug is required at one end and a BS EN 60309-2 connector at the other. The key position should be 6h.

8.5 Tents

608-09-01

BS 7671 does not provide specific requirements for electrical installations in tents, however, electrical installations in tents are common in other countries, especially in permanently erected tents offered by holiday firms, the supply being derived from the park installation. For trailer tents, mains-supply units should be used which incorporate the equipment specified for a caravan, namely a main double-pole isolating switch and a main double-pole RCD (which may be combined), one or more double-pole cbs and socket-outlets as required. Double-pole cb means having overcurrent detection and switching in both poles and not a single-pole cb with a switched neutral. The connecting cable should be securely clamped to the main supply unit and directly connected to it without the use of a plug and inlet. Luminaires and appliances should be of Class II construction.

8.6 Division two, Electrical installations in caravan parks

608 Division two

8.6.1 Supply systems

Electricity supply arrangements may be only TN-S or TT. Where the supply system uses protective multiple earthing (PME), Regulation 9(4) of the Electricity Safety, Quality and Continuity Regulations 2002 prohibits the connection of the neutral to the metalwork of any caravan or boat; this is reflected in BS 7671. Whilst the PME earth may be connected to permanent buildings in the park, such as toilet blocks, the installation feeding the caravans must be part of a TT system having a separate connection to Earth independent of the PME earthing system . This avoids the risks arising from a loss of continuity of the supply PEN conductor when outside the caravan (see 8.2(i)).   608-13-05

The separation of the earthing systems is preferably effected at the main distribution board, where the exposed-conductive-parts connected to each system can be more readily identified and inspected periodically, see Figure 8.1. A main earth electrode for the TT system must be provided nearby, and the resistance areas of the respective electrodes must not overlap, see Figure 8.3. Alternatively, separation may be made at every pitch socket-outlet but this necessitates an earth electrode at each such point, see Figure 8.2.   542-01-04
542-01-09

541-01-02
542-01-09

To ensure disconnection within 0.4 s in the event of an earth fault, distribution circuits may need to be protected by one or more RCDs for either of the methods of earth separation described above. This also applies to TN-S supplies. Distribution RCDs should be time-delayed and have a rated residual operating current of 100 mA or greater, depending on the circuit configuration. Use can be made of 100 mA or greater 'S' type RCDs to BS EN 61008 or BS EN 61009 which will provide discrimination with 30 mA general purpose RCDs to the same standards.   471-08-03

Fig 8.1 Typical site distribution for a PME supply, separation from PME earth at main distribution board

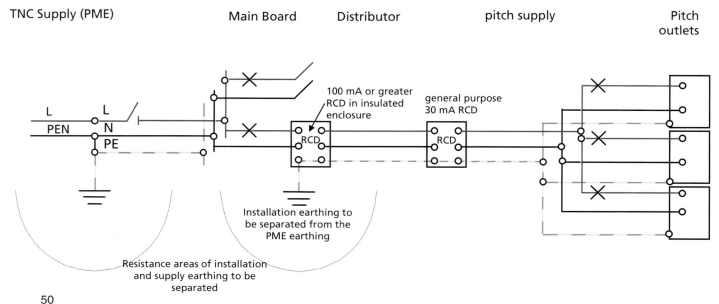

TNC Supply (PME)   Main Board   Distributor   pitch supply   Pitch outlets

L   L
PEN N
PE

100 mA or greater RCD in insulated enclosure

general purpose 30 mA RCD

Installation earthing to be separated from the PME earthing

Resistance areas of installation and supply earthing to be separated

Fig 8.2 Typical site distribution for a PME supply, separation from PME earth at pitch supply point

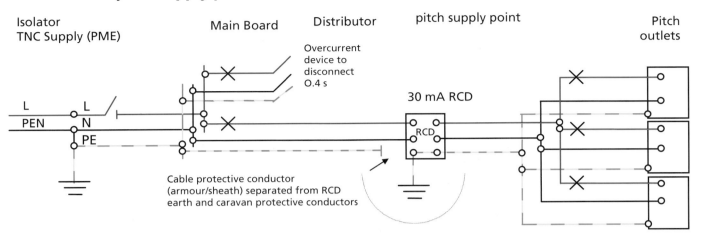

Isolator TNC Supply (PME) · Main Board · Distributor · pitch supply point · Pitch outlets

Overcurrent device to disconnect 0.4 s

30 mA RCD

Cable protective conductor (armour/sheath) separated from RCD earth and caravan protective conductors

8.6.2 Overhead conductors

BS 7671 states a preference for distribution by underground cable. However, overhead distribution systems are allowed provided that all conductors are insulated and so erected as to be unlikely to be damaged by vehicle movements. They are required to be sited at least 2 m beyond the boundary of any pitch. This effectively precludes the use of overhead lines for supplies to pitch socket-outlets, which are normally placed at pitch boundaries.

608-12-01
608-12-03
412-02

8.6.3 Caravan pitches

Dimensions of pitches are not standardised except to the extent that the model standards for touring caravan sites issued under the Caravan Sites and Control of Development Act 1960 states that there shall be not less than 6 metres between caravans and there shall be not less than 3 metres between adjacent units comprising any or all of caravan, awning and car. This requirement dictates minimum pitch dimensions of 11 metres wide and 6 metres deep. However, pitches are often larger and of irregular shape.

8.6.4 Caravan pitch socket-outlets

Caravan pitch socket-outlets are required to comply with BS EN 60309-2 and to have degree of protection IPX4. The current rating is to be not less than 16 A but may be greater if required. Where socket-outlets are grouped in pitch supply equipment, there shall be one socket for each pitch and they shall be connected to the same phase of the supply. To be compatible with the caravan connecting cable, sockets should be two-pole with earthing contact having key position 6 h. (See 8.4.7)

608-13-02

608-13-06

Each socket-outlet must be protected individually by an overcurrent device, which may be a fuse but is more usually a circuit-breaker, and either individually or in groups of not more than three socket-outlets by an RCD having the characteristics specified in Regulation 412-06-02. It may be noted that the CENELEC harmonization

608-13-04
608-13-05

document HD 384.7.708 allows only three sockets to one RCD while the international standard IEC 364-7-708 permits six. This variation does not affect safety from shock but only the reliability of supply to the caravans served. An individual RCCB complying with BS EN 61008-1 or BS 4293, an RCBO complying with BS EN 61009-1 or an SRCD complying with BS 7288 is recommended at every socket-outlet.

Although not included in Section 608 of BS 7671, the supply to permanent homes is preferably made via the fixed wiring through a consumer unit complying with BS EN 60439-3 and either:

- a circuit-breaker complying with BS EN 60898-1 and an RCD complying with BS EN 61008-1, or

- an RCBO complying with BS EN 61009-1.

8.6.5 Separation of electrodes

Fig 8.3 Ground surface potentials around a single rod and three rods in line

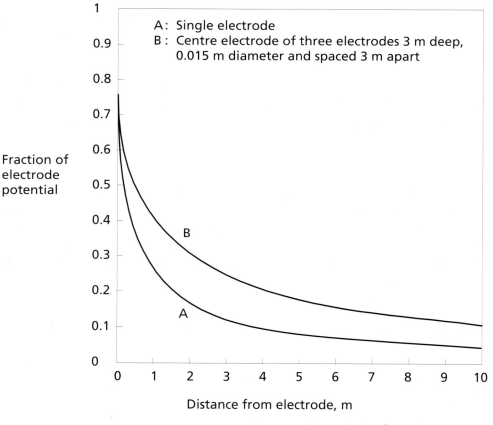

From Fig 8 of BS 7430

Figure 8.3 indicates that effective separation of resistance areas of earth electrodes is achieved if the distance between the electrodes exceeds 10 m.

Chapter 9
ELECTRICAL INSTALLATIONS IN MARINAS

9.1 Introduction

There are no requirements in Part 6 of BS 7671 for Marinas, although Sect 609 section 609 is reserved for this purpose. This guidance is based upon International Electrotechnical Commission Standard IEC 364-7-709, Electrical Installations in Marinas and Leisure Craft and draft CENELEC standard prHD 384-7-709 S1. The notes of this chapter are additional to the recommendations of the draft CENELEC standard.

9.2 Scope

The guidance given applies to the electrical installations of marinas providing facilities for the supply of electricity to leisure craft, in order to provide for standardisation of power facilities.

The requirements do not apply to the electrical installations in offices, workshops, toilets, leisure accommodation etc. which form part of the marina complex, where the general requirements of the Regulations apply.

9.3 The risks

The environment of a marina or yachting harbour is harsh for electrical equipment. The water, salt, and movement of structures accelerate deterioration of the installation. The presence of salt water, dissimilar metals and a potential for leakage currents increases the rate of corrosion. There are also increased electric shock risks associated with a wet environment, by reduction in body resistance and contact with earth potential.

Site investigations should be carried out at an early stage to determine likely maximum wave heights. This is of particular importance in exposed coastal sites. Where marinas have breakwater type pontoons, it is likely that under certain conditions waves will pass over the structure.

The risks specifically associated with craft supplied from marinas include:

i)   Open circuit faults of the PEN conductor of PME supplies raising the potential to true earth of all metalwork (including that of the craft, if connected) to dangerous levels

ii)   Inability to establish an equipotential zone external to the craft

iii)   Possible loss of earthing due to long supply cable runs, connecting devices exposed to weather and flexible cord connections liable to mechanical damage.

Particular requirements to reduce the above risks include:

i)   Prohibition of the connection of exposed- and extraneous-conductive-parts of the craft to a PME terminal

ii)   Additional protection by 30 mA RCDs in both the craft and the marina installation.

9.4   General requirements

Electrical power installations located at marinas should be installed and the equipment so selected as to minimise the risk of electric shock, fire and explosion. Particular regard should be given in the design and construction of such works, to the risk of increased corrosion, movement of structures, mechanical damage, presence of flammable fuel and vapour and the physiological effects of electric shock being increased by a reduction in body resistance and contact of the body with earth potential.

Owing to the harsh working environment of marina installations and potential for abuse and accidental damage by users, particular attention should also be paid to the maintenance and periodic inspection reporting of installations and the general requirements of the Regulations.

9.5   Supplies

Where the supply system is protective multiple earthed (PME), Regulation 9(4) of the Electricity Safety, Quality and Continuity Regulations 2002 prohibits the connection of the neutral to the metalwork of any caravan or boat. While the PME supply may be fed to permanent buildings in the marina, supplies to boats (leisure craft) must have a separate earth system. A TT system having a separate connection with earth, independent of the PME earthing system (Figures 9.3A, 9.3B of this chapter and Figures 8.1 and 8.2 of Chapter 8), will meet this requirement. Alternatively, protection by electrical separation can be adopted, see paragraph 9.8.

This avoids the risks arising from a loss of continuity of the supply PEN conductor.

The separation of the TT earthing system should be effected at the main distribution board where the exposed-conductive-parts connected to each system can be more readily identified and inspected periodically. A main earth electrode for the TT system is to be provided nearby, with no overlap of resistance area with any earthing associated with the PME supply. (See also 8.6.1 of Chapter 8.)

541-01-02

TN-S supplies may be made available both to permanent shore installations and to leisure craft.

The nominal supply voltage of the installation to leisure craft should not exceed 230 V single-phase or 400 V three-phase.

9.6 Protection against direct contact

Protection against direct contact can only be provided by insulation of live parts and/or by barriers or enclosures.

The following methods of protection must not be used:

- protection by obstacles
- protection by placing out of reach.

An RCD complying with BS 4293, BS 7071, BS 7288, BS EN 61008-1 or BS EN 61009-1 may be used to reduce the risk of electric shock caused by direct contact. However, an RCD must not be used as the sole means of protection against direct contact.

471-06-01
471-07-01
412-06-02
412-06-01

9.7 Protection against indirect contact

Protection by non-conducting location should not be used.

471-10-01

Where protection by automatic disconnection of supply is selected:

- for TN systems, only a TN-S arrangement may be used.
- for TT systems, an RCD disconnecting phase and neutral conductors complying with BS EN 61008-1, BS 4293, or BS EN 61009-1, and having the characteristics specified in Regulation 412-06 should be used, including where protection is provided by an onshore isolating transformer.

413-02-19
412-06

Notes

1) Only permanent onshore buildings may use the electricity distributor's PME earthing terminal. For the boat mooring area of the marina this is not permissible, and entirely separate earthing arrangements must be provided. This is generally achieved by the use of a suitably rated RCD complying with BS EN 61008 with driven earth rods or mats providing a TT system for that part of the installation.

2) Marina installations are often of sufficient size to warrant the provision of an 11 kV/ 415 V transformer substation. In these, and sometimes in other, circumstances the electricity distributor may be willing to provide a TN-S supply, which is much more suitable for such installations. If the transformer belongs to the marina, a TN-S system should be installed.

9.8 Isolating transformers

Supplies to craft may be provided from any supply system through isolating transformers. This method has the advantage of reducing electrolytic corrosion and can be used with TN-S and TN-C-S (PME) supplies. See Figure 9.3C.

The isolating transformer must comply with BS EN 60742 Isolating transformers and safety isolating transformers, or the BS EN 61558 series. See Figure 9.3C for typical wiring arrangement with on-shore mounted isolating transformers.

Connection of the protective conductor of the shore supply must not be made to the bonding of the leisure craft. However, the following items must be effectively and reliably connected to a bonding conductor - which, in turn, must be connected to one of the secondary winding terminals of the isolating transformer:

- metal parts of the leisure craft which are in electrical contact with water. If the type of construction does not ensure

continuity, then more than one connection point may be required
- the protective contact of each socket-outlet
- the exposed-conductive-parts of electrical equipment.

Only one craft (socket-outlet) shall be connected to each secondary winding of an isolating transformer.

Note

The isolating transformer isolates the craft installation from the shore, allowing supplies to be taken from multiply earthed networks, and provides some protection against electrolytic corrosion. It does not provide protection against direct or indirect contact, the craft earth is connected to one pole of the secondary isolating transformer.

9.9 Operational conditions and environmental factors

Electrical equipment to be installed on or above jetties, wharves, piers or pontoons must be selected as follows, according to the external influences which may be present. Specific guidance for socket-outlets and distribution boards is given in paragraph 9.11.

External influence	Minimum index of protection
Presence of water splashes	IPX4
Presence of water jets	IPX5
Presence of waves of water	IPX6

9.10 Wiring systems

The following wiring systems should not be used:
- cables supported from or incorporating a catenary (overhead lines)
- cables with aluminium conductors.

Conduit and ducting installations should have suitable apertures or holes and be fixed at an angle sloping away from the horizontal, sufficient to allow for drainage of moisture.

Cables should be selected and installed so that mechanical damage due to tidal and other movement of craft and other floating structures is prevented. To clarify this requirement, cables should be installed in such a manner that they are protected from damage due to:
- displacement by movements of craft or other structures
- friction, tension or crushing
- exposure to adverse temperatures.

See Figure 9.1 for a typical wiring arrangement for offshore pontoons.

At locations where cables are subject to flexing, e.g. bridge ramps, between movable jetties and pontoons, flexible cables should be used, such as:

- cross-linked insulated flexible cables harmonised H07RN-F or H07BN4-F (insulated and sheathed) e.g. cables to tables 14, 15, 16 and 17 of BS 7919 : 2001

- thermosetting insulated flexible cables harmonised type H07Z-K e.g. cables to BS 7211 table 3b within flexible wiring systems.

Notes

1) Cables should be installed in locations where they are protected from physical damage and wherever practicable out of water.

2) Many cable types including PVC-insulated and sheathed cables are not suitable for continuous immersion in water. The suitability of the cable types should be checked with the manufacturers. Floating pontoons are usually manufactured with a service void in them, enclosed and accessible from above, to accommodate cables and water piping.

3) Fixed cables installed permanently under water at a depth of more than 4 m will need to be metal sheathed, e.g. lead.

   Fixed cables not permanently immersed or at a depth of less than 4 m should be armoured and incorporate extruded polythene bedding and outer sheath.

4) Due to the possibility of corrosion, the galvanised steel armouring of cables must not be used wholly or in part as a circuit protective conductor (cpc) on the floating section of marinas. A separate protective conductor should be used which, when in accordance with Regulation 543-01-02, can be common to several circuits if necessary. The armour must still, however, be connected to protective earth.

   543-01-02

5) Equipotential bonding connections must be single-core PVC-insulated to BS 6004 (HAR reference - H07V-R and H07Z-R), or BS 6007 (flexible type), or with an over sheath or further mechanical protection as applicable to the particular location.

6) Conductor colour coding should be in accordance with the requirements of BS 7671 Table 51A. Terminations should be protected against corrosion either by the selection of suitable materials or covering with grease or water-resistant mastic or paint.

   Table 51A

7) Care should be exercised when installing cables to prevent damage from abrasion due to movement between pontoon sections, etc. Cables must be adequately fixed, protected and supported, and if necessary cable types suitable for the flexing movement must be used.

8) Where cables are installed at onshore locations due consideration should be given to the routing, depth of lay and protection especially where heavy traffic and point loads are experienced. Cables should normally be laid above the water table, or cable types suitable for continual immersion used. It is not usually practicable for buried cable duct systems to be made totally watertight. The watertight termination of ducts into drawpits and cable trenches below switchboards is also difficult.

Fig 9.1 Typical wiring arrangement from shore to pontoon

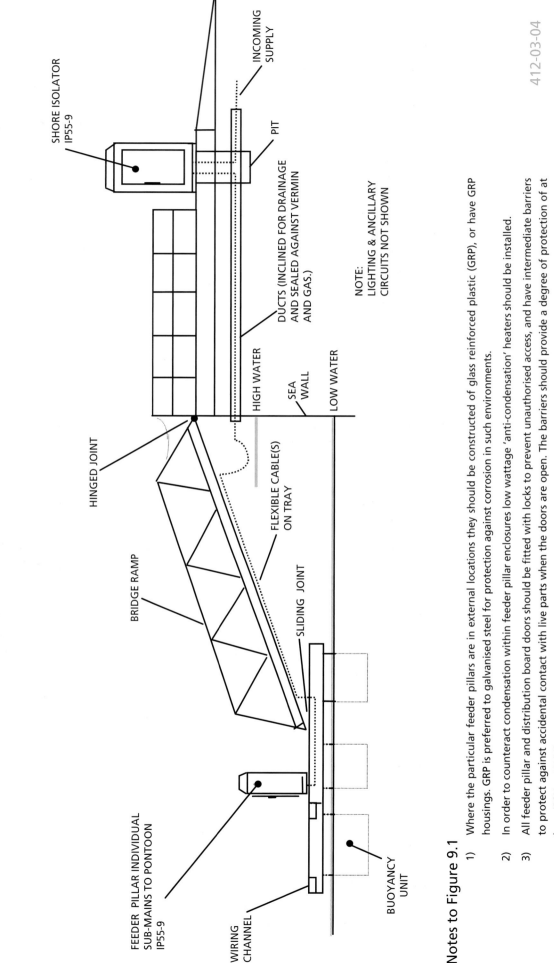

SHORE ISOLATOR IP55-9

INCOMING SUPPLY

PIT

DUCTS (INCLINED FOR DRAINAGE AND SEALED AGAINST VERMIN AND GAS.)

NOTE:
LIGHTING & ANCILLARY CIRCUITS NOT SHOWN

HIGH WATER

SEA WALL

LOW WATER

HINGED JOINT

BRIDGE RAMP

FLEXIBLE CABLE(S) ON TRAY

SLIDING JOINT

FEEDER PILLAR INDIVIDUAL SUB-MAINS TO PONTOON IP55-9

WIRING CHANNEL

BUOYANCY UNIT

412-03-04

Notes to Figure 9.1

1) Where the particular feeder pillars are in external locations they should be constructed of glass reinforced plastic (GRP), or have GRP housings. GRP is preferred to galvanised steel for protection against corrosion in such environments.

2) In order to counteract condensation within feeder pillar enclosures low wattage 'anti-condensation' heaters should be installed.

3) All feeder pillar and distribution board doors should be fitted with locks to prevent unauthorised access, and have intermediate barriers to protect against accidental contact with live parts when the doors are open. The barriers should provide a degree of protection of at least IP2X or IPXXB.

9.11 Distribution boards, feeder pillars and socket-outlets

Distribution boards and feeder pillars mounted outdoors should meet the degree of protection IP44 as a minimum. This will be adequate in sheltered waterways, but the IP code must be selected with reference to the degree of protection necessary for the particular location. The enclosure should be corrosion resistant and give protection against mechanical damage and ingress of dust and sand etc. Distribution boards and feeder pillars supplying marina berths shall be sited in the immediate vicinity of berths. When distribution boards and feeder pillars and their associated socket-outlets are mounted on floating installations or jetties, they should be fixed above the walkway and preferably not less than 1 m above the highest water level. This height may be reduced to 300 mm if appropriate additional measures are taken to protect against the effects of splashing, but care should be taken to avoid creating a low-level obstacle which may cause risk of tripping on the walkway. When mounted on fixed jetties they should be mounted not less than 1 m above the highest water level.

Note

1) While there is a good argument for socket-outlets on feeder pillars and bollards to be mounted at a high level, they may be at risk from damage from the bows of boats which can accidentally overshoot the walkways during berthing. A lower mounting level of 300 mm minimum above the walkway can reduce this risk, but care should be taken to avoid creating a low level obstacle, which may trip the unwary.

Socket-outlets should be mounted as close as possible to the berth to be supplied. A maximum of three socket-outlets may be grouped together in one enclosure. This is to minimise the hazard of long trailing flexes.

Distribution boards and feeder pillars supplying marinas should provide at least one socket-outlet, either single- or three-phase, for each berth. Socket-outlets should be in accordance with BS EN 60309-2 and each outlet should be connected to the circuit protective conductor except where an onshore isolating transformer is used. For isolating transformers, the socket-outlet protective conductor is made to one end of the secondary winding of the isolating transformer and remains separated from the shore earthing - see Figure 9.3C.

Socket-outlets should have the following characteristics, irrespective of the measure of protection against electric shock:

Single-phase socket-outlets

- Rated voltage: 230 V (colour blue)
- Rated current: 16 A
- Key position: 6 h
- Number of poles: 2 plus protective conductor
- Construction: IP44 (minimum)

Three-phase socket-outlets

- Rated voltage: 400 V (colour red)
- Rated current: 16 A

- Key position: 6 h
- Number of poles: 4 plus protective conductor
- Construction: IP44 (minimum)

Where the leisure craft demand is likely to exceed 16 A, provision should be made for outlets of suitable rating.

Socket-outlets or groups of single-phase socket-outlets intended for use on the same walkway or jetty should be connected to the same phase unless fed from isolating transformers.

A notice of durable material is recommended to be placed where practicable adjacent to each group of socket-outlets, bearing indelible, weather proofed and easily legible characters. Alternatively, the notice should be placed in a prominent position or issued to each berth holder. Where shore mounted isolating transformers are <u>not</u> provided the notice should contain the text of Figure 9.2.

Notes

i)   63 A socket-outlets, or larger, are required for some craft. Where necessary, 63 A sockets and greater should have a pilot isolating circuit or mechanical interlock in order to ensure that the load is disconnected before the plug is inserted or withdrawn. BS 7671 allows a plug and socket-outlet to be used as an on-load isolator only for loads up to 16 A.

ii)   Whilst 2 P & E and 4 P & E plugs and sockets are generally used, other configurations may be necessary as in the case of special security circuits indicating unauthorised use of particular socket-outlets on remote monitoring systems.

Except for sockets supplied by isolating transformers each group of socket-outlets should be protected, in groups of not more than 3, by an RCD having a rated residual operating current not exceeding 30 mA (see Figure 9.3A). In any case, the phase and neutral must always be disconnected by the RCD. Each socket-outlet should be provided with means of isolation and shall be protected by an individual overcurrent protective device having a preferred minimum rated current of 16 A, or not more than the current rating of the socket if the rating of this exceeds 16 A.

In TT systems isolation must be all-pole, including the neutral.   461-01-01

Fig 9.2 Notice for shore supplies with direct connection to earth

INSTRUCTIONS FOR ELECTRICITY SUPPLY
BERTHING INSTRUCTIONS FOR CONNECTION TO SHORE SUPPLY
This marina provides power for use on your leisure craft with a direct connection to the shore supply which is connected to earth. Unless you have an isolating transformer fitted on board to isolate the electrical system on your craft from the shore supply system, corrosion through electrolysis could damage your craft or surrounding craft.

ON ARRIVAL

(i)   Ensure the supply is switched off before inserting the craft plug.

(ii)   The supply at this berth is *V, *Hz. The socket-outlet will accommodate a standard marina plug colour * (technically described as BS EN 60309-2, position 6 h).

(iii)   For safety reasons, your craft must not be connected to any other socket-outlet than that allocated to you and the internal wiring on your craft must comply with the appropriate standards.

(iv)   Every effort must be made to prevent the connecting flexible cable from falling into the water if it should become disengaged. For this purpose, securing hooks are provided alongside socket-outlets for anchorage at a loop of tie cord.

(v)   For safety reasons, only one leisure-craft connecting cable supplying one leisure craft may be connected to any one socket-outlet.

(vi)   The connecting flexible cable must be in one length, without signs of damage , and not contain joints or other means to increase its length.

(vii)   The entry of moisture and salt into the leisure-craft inlet socket may cause a hazard. Examine carefully and clean the plug and socket before connecting the supply.

(viii) It is dangerous to attempt repairs or alterations. If any difficulty arises, contact the marina management.

BEFORE LEAVING

(i)   Ensure that the supply is switched off before the connecting cable is disconnected and any tie cord loops are unhooked.

(ii)   The connecting flexible cable should be disconnected **firstly** from the marina socket-outlet and **then** from the leisure-craft inlet socket. Any cover that may be provided to protect the inlet from weather should be securely replaced. The connecting flexible cable should be coiled up and stored in a dry location where it will not be damaged.

*   appropriate figures and colours to be inserted.
        220 - 250 V blue
        380 - 415 V red

Fig 9.3 GENERAL ARRANGEMENTS FOR ELECTRICITY SUPPLY TO LEISURE CRAFT (functional switches not shown)

Fig 9.3A - Connection to mains supply with residual current device

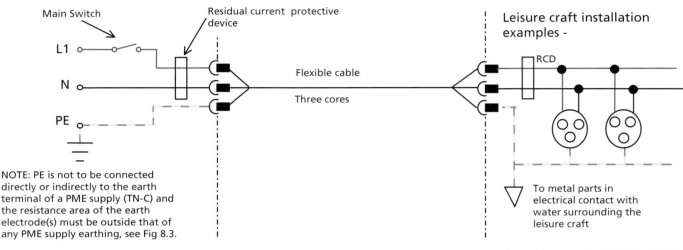

NOTE: PE is not to be connected directly or indirectly to the earth terminal of a PME supply (TN-C) and the resistance area of the earth electrode(s) must be outside that of any PME supply earthing, see Fig 8.3.

From Figure A1 of IEC 364-7-709

Fig 9.3B - Connection to mains supply with three-phase socket-outlet

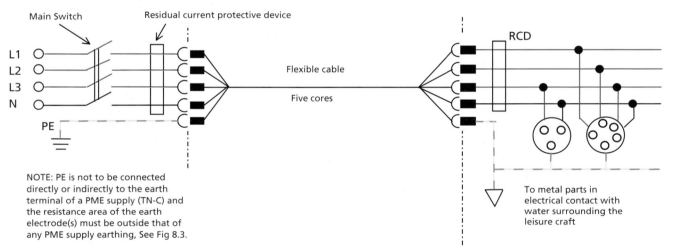

NOTE: PE is not to be connected directly or indirectly to the earth terminal of a PME supply (TN-C) and the resistance area of the earth electrode(s) must be outside that of any PME supply earthing, See Fig 8.3.

Fig 9.3C - On-shore mounted isolating transformer (hull and metal parts bonded)

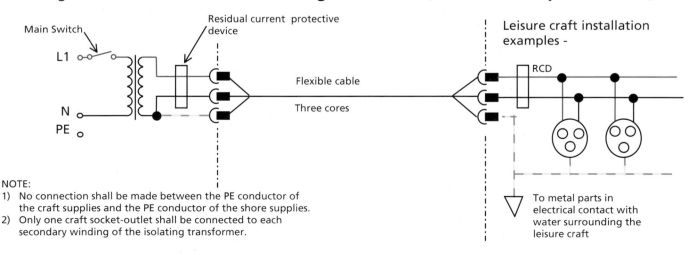

NOTE:
1) No connection shall be made between the PE conductor of the craft supplies and the PE conductor of the shore supplies.
2) Only one craft socket-outlet shall be connected to each secondary winding of the isolating transformer.

9.12 General Notes

1. Pontoon amenity lighting

    It is important that the routes of pontoons and their termination points are clearly delineated.

    The lighting may be controlled by either automatic photo-electric cells or time switches, the former being preferred as they sense poor conditions caused by fog, etc. when natural light is waning.

    Luminaires should be of rugged and watertight construction and should preferably be mounted at low level with the light source facing the walkway, not omnidirectional.

2. Navigational lighting

    The local waterway authority should be consulted in order that all necessary and suitably coloured navigation is provided. The light sources should have an extended life expectancy. Photo-electric cell control is preferred to time switches.

3. Fuelling stations

    The relevant local authority should be consulted in order to ensure that the completed installation complies with its requirements. Where applicable special emergency control facilities should be established onshore. Fuel hoses are required to be non-conducting. Ship/shore bonding cables are not to be used - see The International Safety Guide for Oil Tankers and Terminals 4th edition.

    Electrical equipment in the proximity of fuelling stations should comply with Health and Safety Executive booklet HSG41 Petrol filling stations : Construction and operation. (This is now replaced for new installations by the APEA/IP Guidance for the Design, Construction, Modification and Maintenance of Petrol Filling Stations.).

4. Metering systems

    Metering systems are outside the scope of this guidance note and must be agreed between the designer and the marina owner to provide all necessary electricity consumption information for accurate billing. The meters may be required to be installed locally in the feeder pillars for local direct reading, or may be part of a site wide data network system. The metering system must be fit for the installation and type of use. Functional and safety earthing must be adequate.

    Check metering for the various main sections of the distribution system may be required in order that the marina operator can use this data in establishing tariffs for the resale of electricity. Such equipment must be installed within the main switchgear and feeder pillars, and must be of adequate rating and quality for the duty required. The increased use of items of electrical equipment exhibiting low power factor characteristics, e.g. dehumidifiers, refrigerators, battery chargers, etc., requires that electricity metering should record suitable data to ensure the marina operator does not suffer a loss of revenue. (This particularly applies when kVAh metering is installed by the regional electricity company).

5   Location of equipment

    Due consideration should be given to the location of items of equipment so that they are, as far as practicable, not vulnerable to damage either on or offshore at the marina.

    In the case of onshore areas there will be the need for clear vehicular movement including large mobile boat hoists, transit lorries and cars, etc. The location therefore of feeder pillars and lighting columns requires special attention.

    For marina areas, the lighting columns and power supply feeder pillars should be so positioned that the risk of contact with luggage trolleys etc. and such items as the bowsprit of craft are, as far as practicable, reduced to a minimum. This is particularly important where lighting and power supply equipment has moulded enclosures which are unable to withstand such mechanical forces and impact and may be damaged.

    Site investigations should be carried out at an early stage to determine maximum wave heights which can be experienced. This is of particular importance in exposed coastal sites.

Where marinas have breakwater type pontoons, it is likely that under certain conditions waves will pass over the structure.

6. Routine maintenance and testing

Initial inspection and testing of all electrical systems should be carried out at the completion of the installation, in accordance with the requirements of Part 7 of BS 7671, the recommendations of the IEE's Guidance Note 3 and this guidance note. A periodic inspection and test of all electrical systems should be carried out annually and the necessary maintenance work implemented. If the site is considered to be exposed, or operational experience shows problems (i.e. misuse), the inspection intervals should be reduced to cater for the particular conditions experienced.

All RCDs should be tested regularly by operating the test button and periodically by a proprietary instrument to ensure they conform with the parameters of their relevant product standards e.g. BS 4293, BS EN 61008.

All tests should be tabulated for record purposes and the necessary forms required by Chapter 74 of BS 7671 must be provided by the contractor or persons carrying out the inspection and tests to the person ordering the work.

Chapter 10
MEDICAL LOCATIONS

10.1 Scope

The guidance in this chapter is based on an International Standard (IEC 60364-7-710) published by the International Electrotechnical Committee (IEC) in November 2002 on behalf of TC64. The latter is responsible for the development and updating of the IEC 60364 series of publications covering "Electrical Installations and Protection against Electric Shock".

The particular requirements of IEC 60364-7-710 apply to electrical installations in medical locations where it is necessary to ensure the safety of patients and medical staff. These mainly refer to hospitals, but could also include private clinics, medical and dental practices, healthcare centres and dedicated medical rooms in the work place.

The scope of IEC 60364-7-710 excludes `Medical Electrical Equipment` as they are covered by the IEC 60601 (BS EN 60601) series of publications.

The use of medical electrical equipment can be split into three categories, some examples are listed below:

(a) **Life-support**: Infusion pumps, ventilators and dialysis machines etc;

(b) **Diagnostic**: X-Ray machines, CT Scanners, Magnetic Resonance Imagers, blood pressure monitors, electroencephalograph (EEG) and electrocardiograph (ECG) equipment;

(c) **Treatment**: Surgical diathermy and defibrillators etc.

The increased use of this equipment on patients undergoing acute care requires enhanced reliability and safety of the electrical installations in hospitals to ensure the security of supplies and minimise incidents of electric shock and microshock.

Part 6 of BS 7671 and the chapters of this publication supplement or modify the general requirements of BS 7671. For medical locations, Chapter 56 of BS 7671 Supplies for safety services, is particularly Chap 56 relevant.

10.2 The risks

In medical locations particularly stringent measures are necessary to ensure the safety of patients likely to be subjected to the application of medical electrical equipment.

Shock hazards due to bodily contact with the 50 Hz supply are well known and documented. Currents of the order of 10 mA passing through the human body can result in muscular paralysis followed by respiratory paralysis depending on skin resistances, type of contact, environmental conditions and duration. Eventual ventricular fibrillation can occur at currents just exceeding 20 mA. These findings are listed in IEC/TR2 60479-1 (1994) 'Effects of current on human beings and livestock – general aspects'.

The natural protection of the human body is considerably reduced when certain clinical procedures are being performed on it. Patients under treatment may have their skin resistance broken or their defensive capacity either reduced by medication or nullified while anaesthetised. These conditions increase the possible consequences of a shock under fault conditions.

In patient environments where intracardiac procedures[1] are undertaken, the electrical safety requirements are even stricter, in order to protect the patient against 'microshock'. Patient leakage currents from applied parts introduced directly to the heart can interfere with cardiac function at current levels which would be considered safe under other circumstances. Patient leakage current which can flow into an earthed patient is normally greatest when the equipment earth is disconnected. A limit is set to the amount of leakage current which can flow in the patient circuit when the protective earth conductor is disconnected. Patient leakage currents[2] of the order of 10 μA have a probability of 0.2 % of causing ventricular fibrillation or pump failure when applied through a small area of the heart. At 50 μA (microshock), the probability of ventricular fibrillation increases to the order of 1 % (refer to IEC 60601-1 or BS EN 60601-1).

Note (1) "intracardiac procedure": This is a procedure whereby an electrical conductor is placed within the heart of a patient or is likely to come into contact with the heart, such conductor being accessible outside the patient's body. In this context, an electrical conductor includes insulated wires such as cardiac pacing electrodes or intracardiac ECG electrodes, or insulated tubes filled with conducting fluids (catheter).

Note (2) "Patient's leakage current": Current flowing from a medical electrical equipment applied part via the patient to earth.

Additional to the consideration of risk from electric shock, some electromedical equipment (e.g. life-support equipment, surgical equipment) perform such vital functions that loss of supply would pose an unacceptable risk to the patient. Medical locations where such equipment is used require secure supplies. This has implications not only for the provision of safety (emergency) power supplies (see 10.11), but may also render some conventional protection measures unsuitable. Hence, for example, when protecting circuits supplying critical medical equipment, restrictions are stipulated on the use of RCDs.

10.3 Patient safety

To ensure protection of patients from possible electrical hazards, additional protective measures are recommended in IEC 60364-7-710 to be applied in medical locations. Since the type and description of these hazards can vary according to the treatment being administered, the manner in which a medical room is used necessitates some division into different areas for differing medical procedures. It is proposed to segregate hospital locations into different "Groups". These are:

(a)   Group Zero:
       Medical location where no applied parts[3] are intended to be used.

(b)   Group 1:
       Medical location where applied parts are intended to be used as follows:
       (i)   externally
       (ii) invasively to any part of the body, except where Group 2 applications are intended.

(c)   Group 2:
       Medical location where applied parts are intended to be used in applications such as intracardiac procedures, operating theatres and vital treatment where discontinuity (failure) of the supply can cause danger to life.

Allocation of group numbers and classification of safety services of medical locations shall be made in consultation with the medical staff and health organisation / body responsible for safety. A guide to allocation of group numbers in medical locations is given in Table 10A.

Note (3) Applied part (as defined in IEC 60601-1 / BS EN 60601-1) is the part of the medical electrical equipment which in normal use:
- necessarily comes into physical contact with the patient for the equipment to perform its function, or
- can be brought into contact with the patient, or
- needs to be touched by the patient.

TABLE 10A Examples of allocation of group numbers and classification for safety services of medical locations

A definitive list of medical locations showing their assigned groups is impracticable, as the use to which locations (rooms) might be put may differ. This list is provided for guidance only.

Medical Locations		Group			Class	
		0	1	2	≤ 0.5 s	> 0.5 s ≤ 15 s
1.	Massage room	X	X			X
2.	Bedrooms		X			
3.	Delivery room		X		Xa	X
4.	ECG, EEG, EHG room		X			X
5.	Endoscopic room		Xb			Xb
6.	Examination or treatment room		X			X
7.	Urology room		Xb			Xb
8.	Radiological diagnostic and therapy room, other than mentioned in 21.		X			X
9.	Hydrotherapy room		X			X
10.	Physiotherapy room		X			X
11.	Anaesthetic room			X	Xa	X
12.	Operating theatre			X	Xa	X
13.	Operating preparation room		X	X	Xa	X
14.	Operating plaster room		X	X	Xa	
15.	Operating recovery room		X	X	Xa	X
16.	Heart catheterization room			X	Xa	X
17.	Intensive care room			X	Xa	X
18.	Angiographic examination room			X	Xa	X
19.	Haemodialysis room		X			
20.	Magnetic resonant imaging (MRI)		X			X
21.	Nuclear medicine		X			X
22.	Premature baby room			X	Xa	X

Notes

a) Luminaires and life-support medical electrical equipment which needs power supply within 0.5 s or less.

b) Not being an operating theatre.

Recommendations for medical locations

10.4 Type of system earthing

TN-C systems

The TN-C system is not allowed in medical locations and medical buildings downstream of the main distribution board. This is proscribed to avoid the possible electromagnetic interference to sensitive medical electrical equipment caused by load currents circulating in PEN conductors and parallel paths.

Regulation 8(4) of the Electricity Safety, Quality and Continuity Regulations 2002 prevents the use of combined neutral and earth conductors in any part of a consumer's installation.

10.5 Protection by extra-low voltage: SELV and PELV

Protection by SELV and PELV in medical locations of group 1 and group 2 is limited to 25 V rms a.c. or 60 V ripple free d.c. Also:

(a) when using SELV and/or PELV, protection by insulation of live parts or by barriers or enclosures is necessary even when the nominal voltage does not exceed 25 V rms a.c. or 60 V ripple free d.c.

(b) exposed-conductive-parts of PELV equipment must be connected to the local equipotential bonding conductor connecting all other exposed- and extraneous-conductive-parts (e.g. operating theatre luminaires).

10.6 Protection against electric shock in normal service

Protection by obstacles or placing out of reach is not permitted. Only protection by insulation of live parts and by barriers or enclosures are permitted.

10.7 Protection against indirect contact

Protection by automatic disconnection of supply, by electrical separation or by the use of Class II equipment (or equipment having equivalent insulation) may be used, except as described below.

General

In medical locations of group 1 and 2, where TN, TT and IT systems are installed, the conventional touch voltage U_c shall not exceed 25 V. Additionally, for TN and IT systems, table 41 C of IEC 60364-4-41 shall apply.

TN systems

In medical locations of group 1 and group 2, single-phase final circuits rated up to 32 A shall incorporate residual current devices (RCD) of

Type A or Type B. The maximum residual operating current should be 30 mA and devices used as follows:

(a) Group 1: All circuits

(b) Group 2: Only circuits for
  - the supply to the mechanism controlling the manoeuvrability of operating tables only
  - X-ray units
  - equipment with a rated power exceeding 5 kVA
  - non-critical electrical equipment (non life-support).

TT systems

In medical locations of group 1 and group 2, the above requirements for TN systems apply and in all cases residual current devices shall be used.

Medical IT system [4]

In group 2 medical locations, the medical IT system shall be used for circuits supplying medical electrical equipment and medical systems[5] intended for life support, surgical applications and other electrical equipment located in the "patient environment"[6], excluding equipment listed in TN systems (b) above.

Medical IT systems provide both additional protection from electric shock and improved security of supply under single earth fault conditions.

For each group of rooms serving the same function, at least one separate medical IT system is necessary. The medical IT system shall be equipped with an insulation monitoring device (IMD), in accordance with IEC 61557-8 (BS EN 61557-8) 'Insulation monitoring devices for IT systems'. The IMD shall incorporate both acoustic and visual alarms situated at a suitable place for permanent monitoring by the medical staff. It shall meet the following specific requirements:

- the a.c. internal resistance shall be at least 100 kΩ
- the test voltage shall not be greater than 25 V d.c.
- the test current shall, even under fault conditions, not be greater than 1 mA peak
- indication shall take place at the latest, when the insulation resistance has decreased to 50 kΩ. A test device shall be provided.

Note (4) *IT electrical system having specific requirements for medical applications.*

Note (5) *Combination of items of equipment, at least one of which is an item of medical electrical equipment and inter-connected by functional connection or use of a multiple portable socket-outlet.*

Note (6) *Any volume in which intentional or unintentional contact can occur between patient and parts of the system or between patient and other persons touching parts of the system (for illustration only see Figure 10.2).*

Transformers for the medical IT system

These shall be in accordance with IEC 61558-2-15 (BS EN 61558-2-15): Particular requirements for isolating transformers for the supply of medical locations, with the following additional requirements.

- The leakage current of the output winding to earth and the leakage current of the enclosure, when measured in no-load condition with the transformer supplied at rated voltage and rated frequency, shall not exceed 0.5 mA.

- Single-phase transformers[7] shall be used to form the medical IT systems for portable and fixed equipment and the rated output shall not be less than 0.5 kVA and shall not exceed 10 kVA.

Monitoring of overload and high temperature for the medical IT transformer is required.

See Figure 10.1 for a typical IT system with insulation monitors.

Note [7] *If the supply of three-phase loads via an IT system is required, a separate three-phase transformer shall be provided for this purpose with output line-to-line voltage not exceeding 250 V.*

External Influences

Where appropriate, attention should be given to the prevention of electromagnetic interference.

Fig 10.1 Typical IT system with insulation monitoring

10.1A Theatre Suite

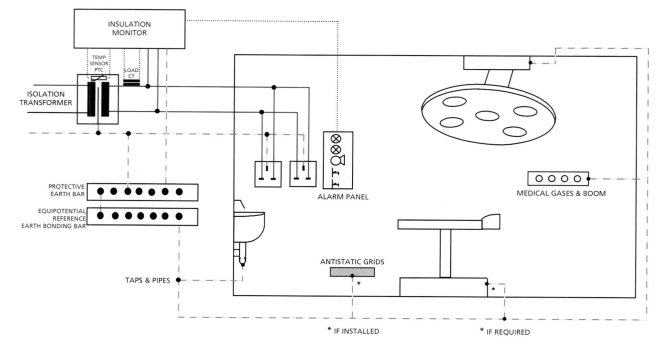

* IF INSTALLED   * IF REQUIRED

10.1B Distribution Network

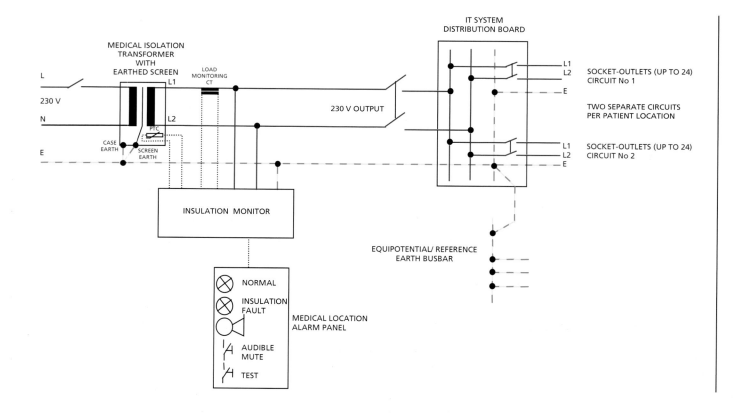

Fig 10.2 Patient environment

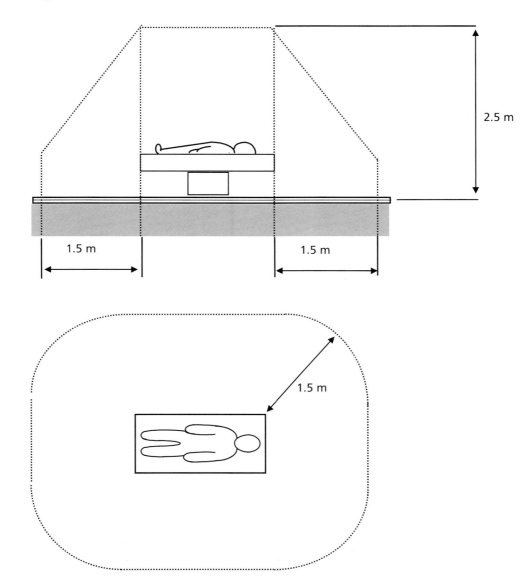

10.8 Supplementary equipotential bonding

In each medical location of group 1 and group 2, supplementary equipotential bonding conductors shall be installed and connected to the equipotential bonding busbar for the purpose of equalizing potential differences between the following parts, located in the "patient environment":

- protective conductors
- extraneous-conductive-parts
- screening against electrical interference fields, if installed
- connection to conductive floor grids, if installed
- metal screen of the isolating transformer, if any.

In medical locations of group 2, the resistance of the conductors, including that of the connections, between the terminals for the protective conductor of socket-outlets and of fixed equipment or any

73

extraneous-conductive-parts and the bonding busbar shall not exceed 0.2 Ω.

The equipotential bonding busbar shall be located in or near the medical location. Connections shall be so arranged that they are clearly visible and readily disconnected.

10.9 Wiring systems

Any wiring system within group 2 medical locations shall be exclusive to the use of equipment and fittings in that location.

10.10 Protection of wiring systems in medical locations of group 2

Overcurrent protection against short-circuit and overload current is necessary for each final circuit. Overload current protection is not allowed in the feeder circuits upstream and downstream of the transformer for the medical IT system. Fuses may be used for short-circuit protection only.

10.11 General requirements for standby power supplies and emergency services

In medical locations, a power supply for safety services[8] is required which, in case of a failure of the normal power supply source, shall be energized to feed specific designated circuits for an adequate duration and within a pre-determined changeover period.

If the voltage at the main distribution board drops in one or several line conductors by more than 10 %, the safety power source should assume the supply automatically. The supply transfer should include a pre-set delay to cater for transient dips in voltage and auto re-closure of circuit-breakers of incoming normal supplies (short-time interruptions), thus avoiding repeated start-up of emergency generator.

For interconnecting cables between the individual components and subassemblies of safety power supply sources, all circuits connecting the power supply source for safety services to the main distribution board should be considered a safety circuit, see Chapter 56 of BS 7671. Chap 56

Note (8) *In UK hospitals, emergency power supplies are synonymous with safety power supplies.*

10.12 Changeover requirements for safety power supply sources

Safety power supplies are split into three classes, depending on changeover requirements:

(a) Power supply for safety services with a changeover period up to 0.5 second:

This requirement mainly applies to luminaires over and around operating theatre tables and other essential luminaires, e.g. endoscopes. The power source should be capable of maintaining them for a minimum period of 3 hours at full design luminance.

(b) Power supply for safety services with a changeover period up to 15 seconds:

This requirement applies to most circuits connected to the "essential supply" electrical system of a hospital. The supply source should be capable of maintaining all essential loads for a minimum period of 24 hours. A time delay of 3 seconds is allowed, to cater for "auto re-closures" of circuit-breakers of normal supplies.

(c) Power supply sources with a changeover period greater than 15 seconds:

This is a recommendation applicable to all other electrical services within a hospital that are not directly associated with life-support activities. They could be connected automatically or manually.

Classification of safety services for medical locations are listed in Table 10B.

TABLE 10B   Classification of safety services for medical locations

(Reference IEC 60364-5-55)

Class 0 (no break)	Automatic supply available at no-break
Class 0.15 (very short break)	Automatic supply available within 0.15 s
Class 0.5 (short break)	Automatic supply available within 0.5 s
Class 15 (medium break)	Automatic supply available within 15 s
Class >15 (long break)	Automatic supply available in more than 15 s

Notes

1 Generally it is unnecessary to provide a no-break power supply for medical electrical equipment. However, certain microprocessor controlled equipment may require such a supply.

2 Safety services provided for locations having differing classifications should meet that classification which gives the highest security of supply. Refer to Table 10A for guidance on the association of classification of safety services with medical locations.

10.13 Socket-outlets and switches

Socket-outlets supplied from the safety power supply source (see 10.11, note 8) shall be readily identifiable.

Socket-outlets and switches shall be installed at a distance of at least 0.2 m horizontally (centre to centre) from any medical gas-outlets.

10.14 Socket-outlets in the medical IT system for medical locations of group 2

At each patient's place of treatment (bedhead) the configuration of socket-outlets, all supplied from the same phase, shall be as follows:

(a)   Either a minimum of two separate circuits feeding socket-outlets shall be installed; or

(b)   each socket-outlet shall be individually protected against overcurrent.

Where circuits are supplied from other systems (TN-S or TT systems) in the same medical location, socket-outlets connected to the medical IT system shall either:

(c)   be of such construction that prevents their use in other systems; or

(d)   be clearly and permanently marked.

10.15 Safety lighting

In the event of mains power failure, emergency lighting shall be provided from a safety power source with necessary minimum illuminance[9] and changeover period not exceeding 15 s. These include escape routes, exit signs, essential services rooms, group 1 and group 2 locations, switchgear and controlgear rooms and locations housing emergency generating sets.

In group 1 medical locations at least one luminaire shall be supplied from the power supply source for safety services. In group 2 medical locations, a minimum of 50% of the lighting shall be supplied from the power sources for safety services.

[9]   *The value for minimum illuminance is determined by national and/or local regulations.*

10.16 Initial and periodic inspection and testing

Certification and reporting

The dates and results of each verification and periodic inspection and test should be recorded in the form specified in Chapter 74 of BS 7671. Chap 74

Initial verification

In addition to Chapters 71 and 72 of BS7671, the following should be carried out: Chap 71 Chap 72

a) Functional test of insulation monitoring devices of medical IT systems and acoustic/visual alarm systems.

b) Measurements to verify that the supplementary equipotential bonding is in accordance with paragraph 10.8.

c) Verification of the integrity of the facilities required by 10.8 for equipotential bonding.

d) Verification of the integrity of the requirements for safety services.

e) Measurements of leakage current of the output circuit and of the enclosure of medical IT transformers in no-load condition.

Periodic inspection and testing

Generally, periodic inspection and testing of items is to be carried out in accordance with Chapter 73 of BS 7671 and the following at the specified intervals: Chap 73

a) Functional testing of changeover devices (every 12 months)

b) Functional test of insulation monitoring devices (every 12 months)

c) Checking, by visual inspection, settings of protective devices (every 12 months)

d) Measurement to verify the supplementary equipotential bonding (every 36 months)

e) Verifying integrity of facilities required for equipotential bonding (every 36 months)

f) Monthly functional testing of:
   – safety services with batteries for 15 min;
   – safety services with combustion engines: until rated running temperature is achieved (12 months for "endurance run");
   – safety services with batteries: capacity test;
   – safety services with combustion engines for 60 min;
   In all cases at least 50% up to 100% of the rated power shall be taken over.

g) Measurements of leakage currents of IT transformers (every 36 months)

h) Checking of the tripping of RCDs at $I_{\Delta n}$ (at intervals of not more than 12 months).

10.17 Recommendations from the UK Health Departments

The Health Departments provide healthcare premises building and engineering guidance through their Health Technical Memoranda (HTM), Health Guidance Notes (HGN) and Health Building Notes (HBN) series of publications. Four HTM's cover low and extra-low voltage electrical technology and safety, and a further HTM covers high voltage systems. These are:

(a)   HTM 2007 - Electrical Services: Supply and Distribution.

(b)   HTM 2011 - Emergency Electrical Services.

(c)   HTM 2014 - Abatement of Electrical Interference.

(d)   HTM 2020 - Electrical Safety Code for High Voltage Systems.

(e)   HTM 2021 - Electrical Safety Code for Low Voltage Systems.

(f)   HGN   - Static discharges.

Note: In Scotland these publications are preceded by `S` e.g. SHTM 2007 and are purchased separately.

Each of HTM's 2007, 2011 and 2014 are published in four separate volumes addressing the different disciplines of 'Management Policy',

'Design Considerations', 'Validation and Verification' and 'Operational Management' in a health care environment.

HTM's 2020 and 2021 contain two volumes each, and they provide information and statutory guidance for those responsible for operating the electrical systems to the requirements of the Electricity at Work Regulations 1989.

Guidance given in these HTM's is complemented by the library of National Health Service Model Engineering Specifications which are also applicable in Scotland.

HGN "Static discharges" provides guidance on prevention of static build-up and methods of controlling its dissipation to earth.

HTM 2007-Electrical Services: Supply and Distribution

This HTM focuses on the legal and statutory requirements, design applications, maintenance and operation of electrical systems in healthcare premises (hospitals).

Its main recommendation emphasises that a hospital electrical distribution system should be designed to provide security of supply and flexibility and safety in operation. The provision of essential and non-essential services and the methodology in designing these distribution systems is also advised.

The "Design Considerations" volume of HTM 2007 recommends that the electrical installation be designed, constructed, commissioned and maintained to the requirements of BS 7671.

HTM 2011 - Emergency Electrical Services

This HTM follows a similar pattern to HTM 2007, dealing with emergency and essential electrical services in hospitals. Its main focus is on standby emergency generating plant, uninterruptible power supplies, emergency lighting and batteries. Similar to HTM 2007, all the recommended design, installation, commissioning and maintenance falls in line with BS 7671.

Chapter 11
HIGHWAY POWER SUPPLIES, STREET FURNITURE and EXTERNAL LIGHTING INSTALLATIONS

Sect 611

11.1 Scope

611-01   By definition, "highway power supplies" include the complete   611-01-01
highway installation comprising distribution boards, final circuits and   Part 2
the street furniture.

The definition of a highway in BS 7671 includes any way over which   Part 2
there is public passage, including verges and bridges. However, the
scope of Section 611 is not so limited. The Section applies to any street   611-01-02
furniture installations on the public way or on private land such as car
parks, public parks, private roads. Equipment to which these
regulations apply includes, but is not restricted to:

Street furniture

(i)   road lighting columns

(ii)   traffic signs

(iii)   footpath lighting

(vi)   traffic control and surveillance equipment

Street located equipment

(i)   bus shelters

(ii)   telephone kiosks

(iii)   car park ticket dispensers

(iv)   advertising signs.

11.2 Protection against electric shock

611-02   Equipment used for highway power supplies is usually located in areas   611-02-01
accessible to the public. In view of this, protection against direct
contact by obstacles and by placing out of reach are not considered
safe i.e. those which should only be applied in a controlled
environment accessible only to skilled persons or instructed persons.
See below for the exceptions for overhead lines.

Overhead lines

Where low voltage overhead lines are constructed to a suitable standard complying with the Electricity Safety, Quality and Continuity Regulations 2002, and maintenance is by skilled persons, the use of protection against direct contact by placing out of reach is permissible. If street furniture or street located equipment is located more than 1.7 m vertically from uninsulated low voltage overhead conductors it is considered that the equipment can be maintained by a suitably instructed person, without danger. Where such equipment is located within 1.7 m of uninsulated overhead conductors maintenance should be carried out by a skilled person specially trained for live working, or measures for protection against direct contact should be provided to prevent contact with the overhead lines, e.g. temporary insulation.

The 1.7 m distance is derived using the definition 'arm's reach' Part 2 including a hand-held tool and is consistent with Electricity Association Engineering Recommendation G.39/1. A person using a platform or ladder will access equipment attached to an overhead line support from below and the zone of reach is limited by the distance from the shoulders. Guidance should also be sought from Engineering Recommendation G.39/1: Model code of practice covering electrical safety in the planning, installation, commissioning and maintenance of public lighting and other street furniture, obtainable from the Electricity Association.

Equipment doors

Doors providing access to electrical equipment contained in street 611-02-02 furniture provide a measure of protection against interference, however, the likelihood of removal or breakage is such that a door less than 2.5 m above ground level cannot be relied upon to provide protection against direct contact. Equipment or barriers within the street furniture are required to prevent contact with live parts by a finger (IP2X or IPXXB).

A street furniture door which has no electrical equipment mounted upon Part 2 it and is not likely to be contacted by wiring is neither an exposed-conductive-part nor an extraneous-conductive-part. Whilst the street lighting column or furniture frame may be an exposed-conductive-part, the door is not, and therefore does not need to be earthed.

Distribution circuits

Items of fixed equipment supplied from a highway distribution circuit are generally in contact with the ground, and they are no more likely to be subject to bodily contact during a fault condition than items of fixed equipment within a building. BS 7671 already recognises a general 5 s disconnection time for fixed equipment. Present-day practice in highway power supplies does not indicate any need to have a shorter disconnection time. Generally, a disconnection time of 5 s is achievable on the circuit up to the controlgear. Where the fault is after the controlgear the ballast would reduce the energy of the fault and the voltage accordingly. 611-02-04

11.3 Devices for isolation and switching

611-03 Each item of street located equipment and street furniture is required to have a local means of isolation. The established practice of using the fuse-carrier as the isolation and switching device is allowed for TN systems provided only instructed persons carry out the work. Formal instruction with the issue of authorisation is appropriate, particularly if the electricity distributor's consent is required. Reference in Regulation 611-03-01 to a suitably rated fuse-carrier will generally limit the use of the fuse-carrier as the main switch to individual items of equipment e.g. one street light, as the fuse-carrier should generally not be used to switch currents exceeding 16 A. 461-01-02
611-03-01
537-05-03
537-05-04

611-03-01

11.4 Protection and identification of cables

611-04 The definitions in regulation 1(5) of the ESQC Regulations are intended to include cables supplying street furniture within the scope of the statutory instrument. Such cables are included within the term "network" and the persons owning or operating such cables are "distributors" as defined. The implications of this are as follows:

(i) In accordance with regulation 14, the cables must be buried at sufficient depth to prevent danger, and they must be protected or marked.

(ii) In accordance with regulation 15(2), the distributor must maintain maps of the cables.

The DTI guidance on the ESQC Regulations gives advice on the methods that duty holders should employ to demonstrate compliance with regulation 14(3) and thereby reduce the risk of injury to contractors or members of the public. Listed in order of preference the methods are:-

(i) Cable installed in a duct with marker tape above.

(ii) Cable installed in a duct only.

(iii) Cable laid direct and covered with protective tiles.

(iv) Cable laid direct and covered with marker tape.

(v) Some other method of mark or indication.

In consideration of the methods by which cables should be marked or protected, duty holders should make allowance for the environment in which the cables are installed and the risks to those who may need to expose and work on or near the cables in future.

The National Joint Utilities Group (NJUG) have agreed colours for ducts, pipes, cables and marker/warning tapes when laid in the public highway. The agreement for highway authority services is reproduced in Table 11A.

Highway distribution circuits mainly consist of cables buried underground. It is impracticable to provide permanent markings to indicate the position of all underground cables, and BS 7671 requires the provision of records or drawings indicating the installed locations. 611-04-01

All cables buried direct are required to have a marker tape placed above them at a depth of 150 mm below finished ground level, additional protection such as ducts or cable tiles would provide the degree of protection required by Regulation 522-06-03 where space is limited. Normally, cables buried direct 450 mm below verges or 750 mm below carriageways will have adequate physical protection.

522-06-03

TABLE 11A   Agreement for highway authority services

Highway Authority Services	Duct	Pipe	Cable	Tape
Street lighting England and Wales	Orange	-	Black	Yellow with black legend
Street lighting Scotland	Purple	-	Purple	Yellow with black legend
Traffic control	Orange	-	Orange	Yellow with black legend
Telecommunications	Light grey	-	Light grey (or black)	Yellow with black legend
Motorways England and Wales				
Communications	Purple	-	Grey	Yellow
Communications power	Purple	-	Black	with black
Road lighting	Orange	-	Black	legend
Scotland				
Communications	Black or grey	-	Black	Yellow with
Road lighting	Purple	-	Purple	black legend

The preferred layout of mains in a 2 m footway prepared by NJUG is reproduced as Figure 11.1.

Fig 11.1   Preferred layout for mains in a 2 m footway for new works

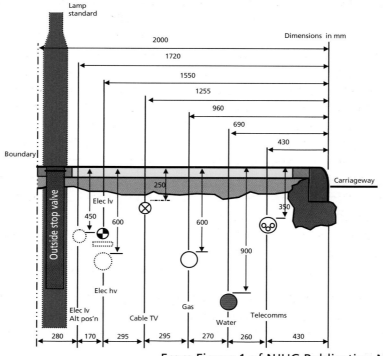

From Figure 1 of NJUG Publication No 7

11.5 External influences

Highway equipment suffers from external influences which include condensation, corrosion, vibration and vandalism, and the designer should take account of such factors in the selection of equipment. Where lamp controlgear is present the heat generated by the equipment coupled with adequate ventilation will generally be sufficient to combat the effect of condensation and corrosion. However, in other situations the provision of a low wattage heater may be necessary to limit the effects of condensation and extend useful life. Luminaires and other electrical equipment should be secured in a manner to withstand vibration caused by wind and vehicles. All enclosures should be provided with access doors which can only be opened with a tool and should be resistant to vandalism.

512-06-01

Equipment is required to have a degree of protection against ingress of solid objects and water after erection of at least IP 33.

611-05-02

It is the aim to reduce risks associated with imported and exported faults. Equipotential bonding to adjacent metallic structures could introduce a hazard during fault conditions by transmitting dangerous voltages above earth. Therefore adjacent metallic structures should not be bonded to the circuit protective conductor or main earthing terminal without careful consideration of the danger.

611-02-05

11.6 Temporary supplies

Before connecting any temporary load the requirements which deal with increase of load must be considered.

130-07-01

It is important to protect against damage to the existing permanent equipment in the base compartment of an item of street furniture when connecting up a temporary installation. The connection of temporary loads directly to existing fixed installations can lead to damage to the cores of permanent wiring cables. Where it is envisaged that temporary connections will be re-used in the future, it is considered preferable to fit a socket-outlet to feed the temporary load, which can then be left in position after the load has been disconnected and re-used at a later date. Also, it is intended that access to the base compartment of street furniture and street located equipment by unauthorised persons shall not be made significantly easier by the addition of a temporary supply unit. Whatever the type of unit used, it must be capable of being secured in place by, for example, stainless steel banding and must totally cover the base compartment aperture. It is recommended that a socket-outlet be mounted inside such units, preferably behind a lockable access door, to facilitate connection to and disconnection from the unit of the temporary load, without having to remove the unit itself.

611-06

Part 2

It is recommended that temporary supply units which are designed to fit externally over the base compartment aperture of street furniture, are manufactured from corrosion-resistant material and fitted with suitable seals to prevent ingress of water.

Temporary power supplies are required to be generally in accordance 611-06-01 with the requirements for construction sites. This can be considered to imply a requirement for reduced disconnection times, and may require the installation of an RCD or a 110 V centre-tapped to earth transformer, see Figure 11.2.

Fig 11.2 Temporary supplies from columns - alternative arrangements

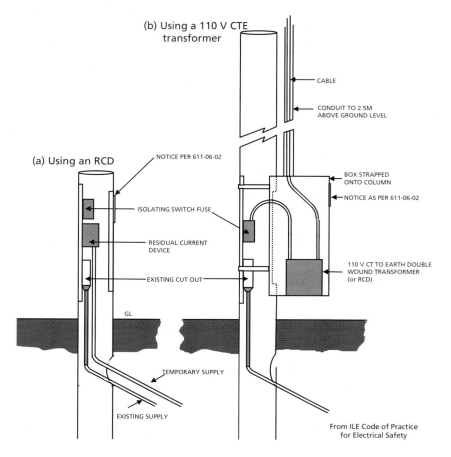

11.7 Temporary decorative lighting

It is recommended that any decorative lighting (such as Christmas tree lights) within reach of the general public be supplied by SELV. Such equipment is readily available and suitable for indoor and outdoor use.

Decorative lighting installed out of reach of the public may be supplied at 230 V. If it is inaccessible it will not normally require RCD protection. However, the risk of electric shock during normal operation and maintenance should always be assessed for each installation. If such lighting is essential for illumination the risk from sudden loss of lighting caused by an RCD tripping should be compared with the risk from electric shock; where RCD protection is considered necessary under such conditions, the risk of unwanted tripping should be minimised by splitting circuits, using time-delayed devices, etc. as described in paragraph 5.3 in Chapter 5.

11.8 Class II equipment

Some items of street furniture such as some parking meters and some telephone kiosks are of Class II construction. Regulation 611-02-06 requires that any metal enclosure of such equipment, such as the telephone kiosk structure, is not connected to the earthing terminal so that any problems associated with open-circuit PEN conductors of PME supplies are avoided (see also 413–03–09). An earth terminal is required to be provided (see Regulation 471-08-08) for Class II luminaires fitted to Class I columns, in case the Class II luminaire is replaced by a Class I luminaire. Class II columns will need an earth terminal to provide for the connection of Class I luminaires.

611-02-06

413-03-09
471-08-08

11.9 External lighting installation

The requirements of Section 611 and the guidance of this chapter for highway power supplies, street furniture and street located equipment can usefully be applied to lighting installations for parks, gardens, public places, sports areas, illumination of monuments and floodlighting.

611

Protection by automatic disconnection of supply

In the case of installations supplied by TT systems, if the earth electrode is of sufficiently low resistance, protection against indirect contact by disconnection by fuses or circuit-breakers is preferred. The use of a single residual current protective device at the origin of the installation in the event of a single fault can cause the disconnection of the whole lighting installation and create a safety risk for the users. If RCDs are to be used the number of circuits and the need for segregation of these circuits in the event of a fault must be considered.

Metallic structures such as fences, grids, etc that are in the proximity of but are not part of the external lighting installation need not be connected to the earthing terminal.

Selection of equipment (degrees of protection)

Equipment generally should have, by construction and/or by installation, at least the degree of protection IP 33, although in some circumstances due to operational or cleaning conditions higher degrees of protection may be required.

11.10 References

BS 5489, Code of Practice for Road Lighting.

NJUG Publication 7, Recommended positioning of utilities mains and plant for new works.

Electricity Association Engineering Recommendation G39/1 Model code of practice covering electrical safety in the planning, installation, commissioning and maintenance of public lighting and other street furniture.

Institution of Lighting Engineers Code of Practice for Electrical Safety in Public Lighting Operations.

Chapter 12
Solar photovoltaic (PV) power supply systems
IEC
60364-7-712

12.1 Scope

There is no section of BS 7671 at this time providing requirements for solar photovoltaic power supply systems. The guidance given in this chapter is based on the requirements of IEC 60364-7-712: Requirements for special installations or locations – solar photovoltaic (PV) power supply systems.

The particular requirements of this part of IEC 60364 apply to electrical installations of PV power supply systems which will only work when connected in parallel with an electricity supply. The requirements in this section are not intended for PV systems for stand-alone operation.

The requirements are for PV systems assembled from items of equipment, not supplied as a complete unit.

12.2 The Electricity Safety, Quality and Continuity Regulations 2002

The solar photovoltaic (PV) power supply systems described in this chapter are required to meet the requirements of the Electricity Safety, Quality and Continuity Regulations 2002 as they are embedded generators.

Where the output does not exceed 16 A per phase they are small-scale embedded generators (SSEG) and are exempted from certain of the requirements provided that:-

(i) the equipment should be type tested and approved by a recognised body,

(ii) the consumer's installation should comply with the requirements of BS 7671,

(iii) the equipment must disconnect itself from the distributor's network in the event of a network fault, and

(iv) the distributor must be advised of the installation before or at the time of commissioning.

The requirements of the ESQC Regulations for small-scale embedded generators are discussed more fully in Chapter 18.

Installations will need to meet the requirements of Electricity Association Engineering Recommendation G83, Recommendations for the connection of small-scale embedded generators (up to 16 A per phase) in parallel with the public low voltage distribution network.

12.3 Normative references

The following IEC standards are referred to in this recommendation.

IEC 60904-3: Photovoltaic devices – Part 3: Measurement principles for terrestrial photovoltaic (PV) solar devices with reference spectral irradiance data

EC 612215: Crystalline silicone terrestrial photovoltaic (PV) modules – Design qualification and type approval.

Standards for equipment are being developed by IEC Committee TC 82.

12.4 Definitions

(See also Figures 12.1 and 12.2)

PV cell

basic PV device which can generate electricity when exposed to light such as solar radiation

PV module

smallest completely environmentally protected assembly of interconnected PV cells

PV string

circuit in which PV modules are connected in series, in order for a PV array to generate the required output voltage

PV array

mechanically and electrically integrated assembly of PV modules, and other necessary components, to form a DC power supply unit

PV array junction box

enclosure where all PV strings of any PV array are electrically connected and where protection devices can be located if necessary

PV generator

assembly of PV arrays

PV generator junction box

enclosure where all PV arrays are electrically connected and where protection devices can be located if necessary

PV string cable

cable connecting PV modules to form a PV string

PV array cable

output cable of a PV array

PV DC main cable

cable connecting the PV generator junction box to the DC terminals of the PV inverter

PV inverter

device which converts DC voltage and DC current into AC voltage and AC current

PV supply cable

cable connecting the AC terminals of the PV inverter to a distribution circuit of the electrical installation

PV AC module

Integrated module/invertor assembly where the electrical interface terminals are AC only. No access is provided to the DC side

PV installation

erected equipment of a PV power supply system

Standard test conditions (STC)

test conditions specified in IEC 60904-3 for PV cells and modules

Open-circuit voltage under standard test conditions $U_{OC\ STC}$

voltage under standard test conditions across an unloaded (open) PV module, PV string, PV array, PV generator, or on the DC side of the PV inverter

Short-circuit current under standard test conditions $I_{SC\ STC}$

short-circuit current of a PV module, PV string, PV array or PV generator under standard test conditions

DC side

part of a PV installation from a PV cell to the DC terminals of the PV inverter

AC side

part of a PV installation from the AC terminals of the PV inverter to the point of connection of the PV supply cable to the electrical installation

Simple separation

separation provided between circuits or between a circuit and earth by means of basic insulation

12.5 Protection for safety

(1) Protection against electric shock

Chap 41

PV equipment on the DC side is to be considered energized, even when the system is disconnected from the AC side.

The selection and erection of equipment shall facilitate safe maintenance and shall not adversely affect provisions made by the manufacturer of the PV equipment to enable maintenance or service work to be carried out safely.

(2) Protection against both direct and indirect contact

411

Protection by extra-low voltage: SELV and PELV

411-02
471-14

For SELV and PELV systems, $U_{OC\ STC}$ replaces U_n and shall not exceed 120 V DC.

(3) Fault protection

413

(a) *Protection by automatic disconnection of supply*

413-02

NOTE Protection by automatic disconnection of supply on the DC side requires special measures which are under consideration.

On the AC side, the PV supply cable shall be connected to the supply side of the protective device for automatic disconnection of circuits supplying current-using equipment.

Where an electrical installation includes a PV power supply system without at least simple separation between the AC side and the DC side, an RCD installed to provide fault protection by automatic disconnection of supply shall be type B to IEC 60755 amendment 2.

Where the PV power supply inverter by construction is not able to feed DC fault currents into the electrical installation an RCD of type B to IEC 60755 amendment 2 is not required.

(b) *Other protective measures*

Protection by use of Class II or equivalent insulation should preferably be adopted on the DC side.

413-03

Protection by non-conducting location is not permitted on the DC side.

413-04

Protection by earth-free local equipotential bonding is not permitted on the DC side.

413-05

(4) Protection against overload on the DC side

NOTE: For PV cables on the DC side not complying with the paragraphs below the requirements of Chapter 43 of BS7671 apply for overload protection.

Overload protection may be omitted to PV string and PV array cables when the continuous current-carrying capacity of the cable is equal to or greater than 1.25 times $I_{SC\,STC}$ at any location.

473-01-03

Overload protection may be omitted to PV main cables when the continuous current-carrying capacity of the PV main cable is equal to or greater than 1.25 times $I_{SC\,STC}$ of the PV generator.

473-01

NOTE: These requirements are only relevant for protection of the cables. Also see the manufacturer's instructions for protection of the PV modules.

(5) Protection against short-circuit current

434-01

The PV supply cable shall be protected against short-circuit current by an overcurrent protective device installed at the connection to the AC mains.

Protection against electromagnetic interference (EMI)

To minimize voltages induced by lightning, the area of all wiring loops shall be kept as small as possible.

12.6 Isolation and switching

Isolation

To allow maintenance of the inverter, means of isolating the PV inverter from the DC side and the AC side shall be provided.

Note: Further requirements with regard to the isolation of a PV installation operating in parallel with the public supply system are given in Section 551-07 of BS 7671.

12.7 Selection and erection of electrical equipment

Part 5

(1) Compliance with standards

PV modules shall comply with the requirements of the relevant equipment standard, e.g. IEC 61215 for crystalline PV modules. PV modules of Class II construction or with equivalent insulation are recommended if $U_{OC\ STC}$ of the PV strings exceeds 120 V DC.

The PV array junction box, PV generator junction box and switchgear assemblies shall be in compliance with IEC 60439-1.

(2) Operational conditions and external influences

Electrical equipment on the DC side shall be suitable for direct voltage and direct current.

PV modules may be connected in series up to the maximum allowed operating voltage of the PV modules or the PV inverter, whichever is lower. Specifications for this equipment shall be obtained from the equipment manufacturer.

If blocking diodes are used, their reverse voltage shall be rated for 2 x $U_{OC\ STC}$ of the PV string. The blocking diodes shall be connected in series with the PV strings.

As specified by the manufacturer, the PV modules shall be installed in such a way that there is adequate heat dissipation under conditions of maximum solar radiation for the site.

When installing PV modules the installer shall follow the manufacturer's instructions for mounting so that adequate heat dissipation is provided under the conditions of maximum solar radiation to be expected. Such instructions are required by the equipment standard.

(3) Wiring systems

Selection and erection in relation to external influences

PV string cables, PV array cables and PV DC main cables shall be selected and erected so as to minimize the risk of earth faults and short-circuits.

NOTE: This may be achieved for example by reinforcing the protection of the wiring against external influences by the use of single-core sheathed cables.

Wiring systems shall withstand the expected external influences such as wind, ice formation, temperature and solar radiation.

(4) Switchgear

Devices for isolation and switching

In the selection and erection of devices for isolation and switching to be installed between the PV installation and the public supply, the public supply shall be considered the source and the PV installation shall be considered the load.

A switch disconnector shall be provided on the DC side of the PV inverter.

All junction boxes (PV generator and PV array boxes) shall carry a warning label indicating that active parts inside the boxes may still be live after isolation from the PV inverter.

The DTI notes of guidance on the ESQC Regulations advise that the means of disconnection should preferably be by mechanical separation of contacts. However, a suitably rated solid-state switching device is permitted by the DTI provided it is equipped with fail-safe monitoring to ensure that the phase to neutral voltage on the mains side of the device reduces to less than 50 volts within 0.5 seconds of the device failing to operate when required to do so. The means of isolation of the generating plant (for the purposes of working either on the consumer's system or the distributor's network as required) should be by an accessible all-phases and neutral manually-operated electromechanical isolating switch in all circumstances.

12.8 Earthing arrangements and protective conductors

Where equipotential bonding conductors are installed, they shall be parallel to and in as close a contact as possible with DC cables and AC cables and accessories.

Types of system earthing

Earthing of one of the live conductors of the DC side is permitted, if there is at least simple separation between the AC side and the DC side.

NOTE: Any connections with earth on the DC side should be electrically connected so as to avoid corrosion.

Fig 12.1 PV installation - general schematic, one array

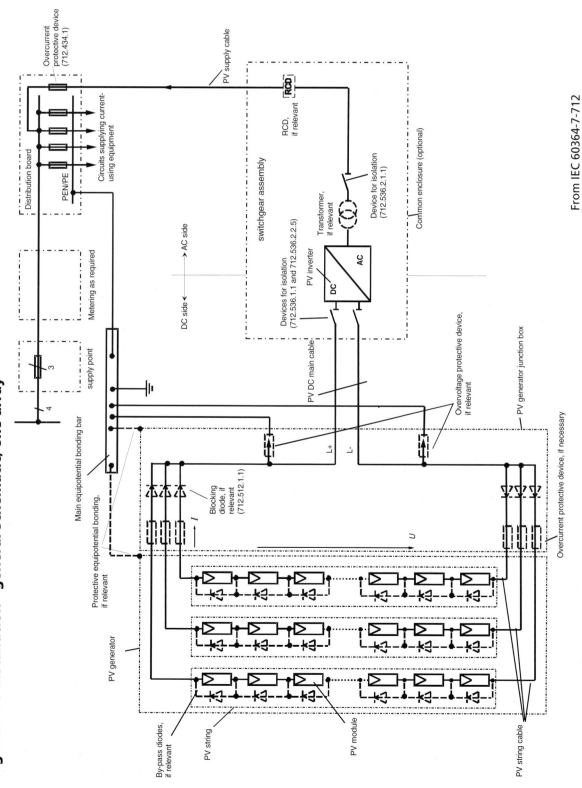

From IEC 60364-7-712

Fig 12.2 PV installation - example with more than one array

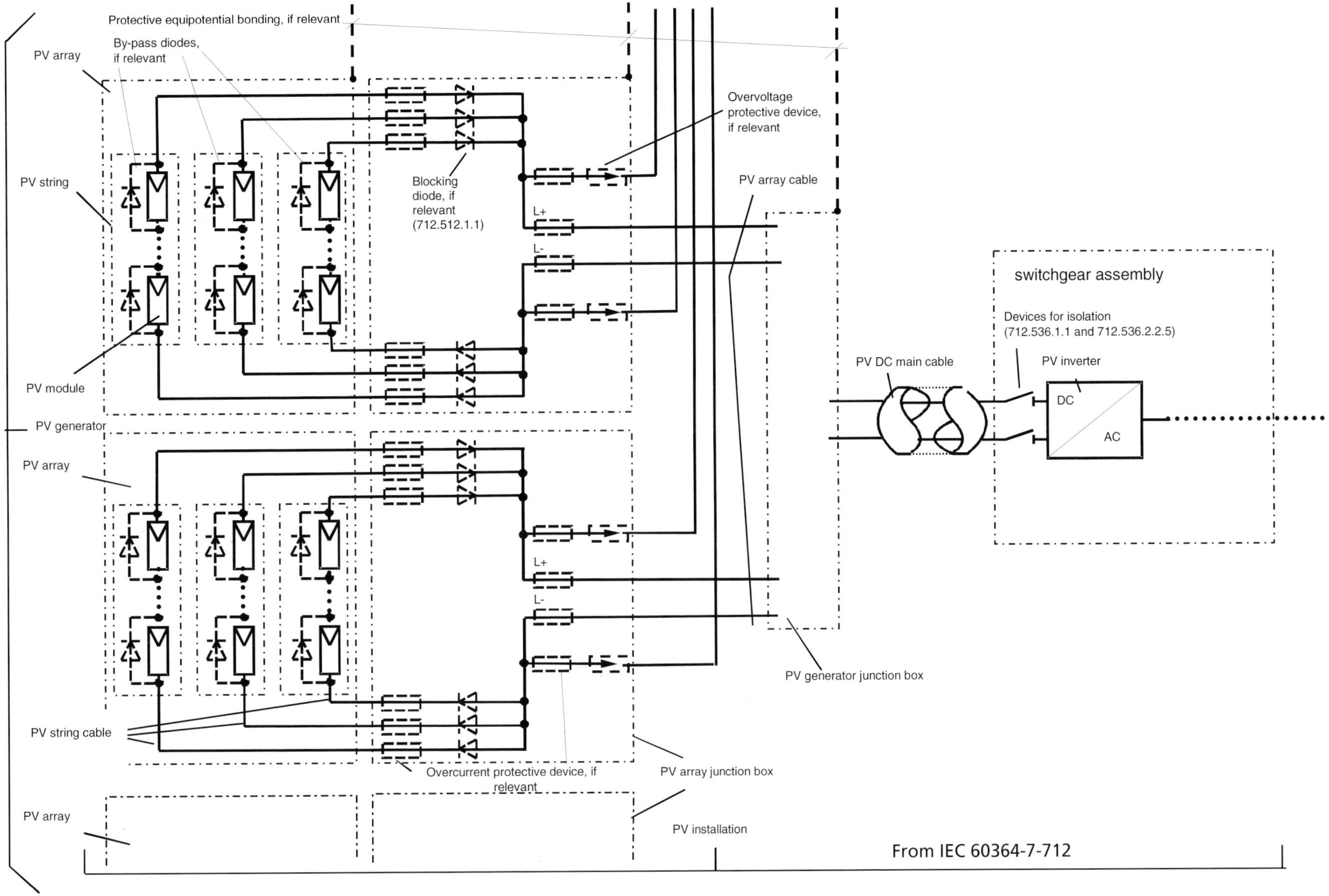

switchgear assembly

Devices for isolation (712.536.1.1 and 712.536.2.2.5)

PV inverter

DC

AC

PV DC main cable

PV generator junction box

PV array cable

Overvoltage protective device, if relevant

L+

L-

PV array junction box

PV installation

Overcurrent protective device, if relevant

Blocking diode, if relevant (712.512.1.1)

Protective equipotential bonding, if relevant

By-pass diodes, if relevant

PV array

PV string

PV module

PV generator

PV array

PV string cable

PV array

From IEC 60364-7-712

93

Chapter 13
EXHIBITIONS, SHOWS AND STANDS

13.1 Introduction

There is no section in Part 6 of BS 7671 for exhibitions, shows and stands. The guidance provided in this chapter is based on IEC Publication 60364-7-711 and the draft CENELEC proposals prHD 384.4.7.711 S1:2002.

13.2 Scope

This chapter is concerned with temporary electrical installations in exhibitions, shows and stands. Such installations may be installed indoors or outdoors within permanent or temporary structures. It does not apply to the electrical installation of the building, if any, in which the exhibition, shows or stands take place.

13.3 The risks

The particular risks associated with exhibitions, shows and stands are those of electric shock and fire. These arise from :

1.   the temporary nature of the installation

2.   lack of permanent structures

3.   severe mechanical stresses

4.   access to the general public.

Because of these increased risks additional measures are recommended as described in the following sections.

13.4 Protection against electric shock

Protective measures against direct contact by means of obstacles and by placing out of reach are not acceptable. 471-06 471-07

Protective measures against indirect contact by non-conducting location and by earth-free equipotential bonding should not be used. 471-10 471-11

Protection by automatic disconnection of supply

Because of the practical difficulties of bonding all accessible extraneous-conductive-parts, a TN-C-S (PME) system is not appropriate for temporary and/or outdoor installations. A TN-S system would be acceptable if such a supply was available from the distributor. It is most likely and preferable for TT systems to be adopted. (The IEC standard allows neither TN-C nor TN-C-S systems) 413-02

Choice of protective measure as a function of external influence

Distribution circuits

Where there is increased risk of damage to cables, disconnection of supply should be provided by a residual current device having a rated residual operating current not exceeding 500 mA. To provide for discrimination with RCDs protecting final circuits, the RCD should be type S to BS EN 61008 or BS EN 61009 or time-delayed to BS 4293. See Figure 13.

The installation of RCDs will also increase the protection against the risk of fire arising from leakage currents to earth.

Fig 13 Exhibition/show distribution with standby generator

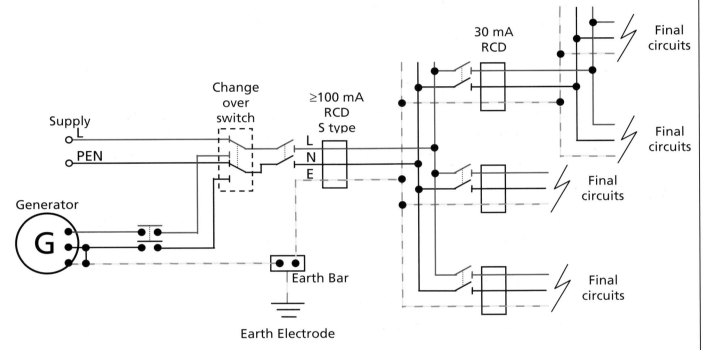

Note to Figure 13:
Regulation 21 of the ESQC Regulations has requirements for switched alternative sources of energy, see 13.10

Socket circuits

All circuits for socket-outlets rated up to 32 amps, and all final circuits other than for emergency lighting, shall be protected by an RCD with a total residual operating current not exceeding 30 mA.   605-03-01

Other circuits

Final circuits, other than emergency lighting, which are accessible to the general public should also be protected by a 30 mA RCD. However, consideration has to be given to the hazards of loss of lighting in such a public place, particularly when crowded. Lighting of such areas should always be on at least two separate circuits with separate RCDs, and should preferably be out of reach of the general public.

Bonding of vehicles, wagons and caravans

Extraneous-conductive-parts on vehicles, wagons, caravans, metallic containers should be bonded to the protective conductor of the installation, in more than one place if necessary. The nominal cross-sectional area of conductors used for this purpose should be not less than 4 mm². 608-03-04 547-03-02

If the vehicle etc. is made of substantially insulating material, these requirements do not apply to metal parts which are unlikely to become live in the event of a fault. 608-03-04

13.5 Protection against thermal effects

Chapter 42 There is often an increased risk of fire and burns in temporary locations. It is important to comply with all the requirements of Chapter 42.

Where SELV or PELV installations are used, the insulation is required to be as for standard 230 volt supplies, applying test voltages of 500 volts d.c. and providing protection of least IP4X or IPXXD.

Protection against fire

Installation designers must bear in mind that stored materials may present a particular hazard in such a location, particularly fodder, cardboard boxes etc.

Motors which are automatically or remotely controlled and are not continuously supervised should be fitted with manual reset devices for protection against excess temperature, accessible only to skilled persons. 482-02-11 552-01-02

Lighting

Lighting equipment such as incandescent lamps, spotlights, projectors and other apparatus or appliances with high temperature surfaces should, in addition to being suitably guarded, be arranged well away from combustible materials such as to prevent contact. Equipment should be installed on location in accordance with relevant standards and manufacturer's instructions. 422-01-01 482-02-13

Show-cases and signs should be constructed from materials having adequate heat resistance, mechanical strength, electrical insulation and ventilation, taking account of the combustibility of exhibits in relation to the heat generated. The manufacturer's instructions must be complied with.

Where there is a concentration of electrical equipment, including luminaires that might generate considerable heat, adequate ventilation must be provided.

13.6 Isolation

Sect 461 Every separate temporary structure, such as vehicles, stands, or units, intended to be occupied by one specific user, and each distribution circuit supplying outdoor installations, should be provided with its own readily accessible and properly identifiable means of isolation. Switches, circuit-breakers and residual current devices etc. considered 131-14-01 460-01-01 461-01-05 suitable for isolation by the relevant standard or the manufacturer may be used.

13.7 Measures of protection against overcurrent

Chapter 43 All circuits should be protected against overcurrent by a suitable protective device located at the origin of the circuit. Exceptions to this rule are not permitted, even where circuits are not liable to overload. 431-01-01

13.8 Selection and erection of equipment

Equipment, particularly switchgear and fusegear, must be mounted away from locations that may not be weatherproof. Tent poles etc. which may be suitable for mounting switchgear are often the weak point in the weather tightness of temporary structures. 512-06-01

Control and protective switchgear should be placed in closed cabinets which can only be opened by a key or tool, except those parts which are designed and intended to be operated by ordinary persons (a person who is neither a skilled person nor an instructed person). Part 2

The means of isolation for each stand or exhibit etc. should not be locked away and should be readily accessible and obvious to the stand user.

13.9 Wiring systems

Chapter 52 Particular care must be paid to the selection and installation of cables to ensure that the mechanical protection, insulation, heat resistance and current-carrying capacity are sufficient for the conditions that are likely to be encountered. 522 523

Mechanical protection or armoured cables should be used wherever there is a risk of damage, and flexible cords should not be laid in areas accessible to the public unless they are protected against mechanical damage.

Underground cables are susceptible to damage by structure support pins which may be up to 1 m in length. Exhibitors must be advised of the presence of cables and if necessary the cable route marked. The general rules for buried cables must be followed, see also paragraph 16.2 in Chapter 16.

Types of wiring system

Where no fire alarm is installed in a building used for exhibitions etc. cables should be :

- flame retardant low smoke complying with BS EN 50265-1, BS EN 50266-2-4 and BS EN 50268-2, or

- enclosed in trunking, ducting or conduit complying with the resistance to flame propagation requirements of BS EN 50085-1 or BS EN 50086-1.

Electrical connections
526

Joints should not be made in cables, except as a connection into a circuit. 133-01-04

Conductor connections should be within an enclosure providing a degree of protection of at least IP4X or IPXXD and the enclosure should incorporate a cable anchorage. 422-01-04

Lighting installations

Luminaires mounted below 2.5 m (arm's reach) from floor level or otherwise accessible to accidental contact need to be firmly and adequately fixed and so sited as to prevent risk of injury to persons or ignition of materials.

131-05-02

Insulation piercing lampholders should not be used unless the cable and lampholders are compatible and providing the lampholders are not removable once fitted to the cable.

Outdoor lighting installations shall be constructed to International Protection Code IP33 or better. Extra-low voltage lighting systems shall comply with EN 60598-2-23.

Electric discharge lamps

Installation of any luminous sign or lamp on a stand or exhibit with a supply voltage U_o higher than 230 volts a.c. should comply with the following :

- the sign or lamp should be installed out of reach or should be adequately protected to reduce the risk of injury to persons
- the facia or stand fitting material should be non-flame-propagating
- a separate circuit should be used to supply such signs, lamps or exhibits and should be controlled by an emergency switch located in an accessible and visible position and labelled
- signs and high voltage discharge lamp installations should comply BS 559 : 1991 Specification for electric signs and high voltage luminous-discharge-tube installations.

Electric motors

Where an electric motor might give rise to a hazard the motor must be provided with an effective means of isolation on all poles and if necessary an emergency stop, and the means should be adjacent to the motor it controls.

131-14-02

Extra-low voltage transformers and electronic converters

A manual reset protective device should be fitted to the primary and secondary circuit of each transformer.

Particular care should be taken to install ELV transformers out of reach of the public and adequate ventilation should be allowed for. Access should be provided for skilled or instructed persons for testing and for protective device maintenance.

Electronic converters should conform with BS EN 61046.

Socket-outlets

An adequate number of socket-outlets should be installed to allow user requirements to be met safely.

553-01-07

Floor mounted sockets should preferably not be installed but where their use is unavoidable, they should be adequately protected from mechanical damage and ingress of water.

Flexible cables or cords shall not be laid in areas accessible to the public unless they are protected against mechanical damage.

13.10 Generators

551 Installations incorporating generator sets shall comply with Section 551 of BS 7671. Where a generator is used to supply the temporary installation using a TN or TT system, it must be ensured that the installation is earthed, preferably by separate earth electrodes. For TN systems all exposed-conductive-parts should be bonded back to the generator. The neutral conductor and/or star point of the generator should be connected to the exposed-conductive-parts of the generator and reference earthed. See Figure 13.

Part VI of the ESQC Regulations provides requirements for generation. Regulation 21 has requirements for switched alternative sources of energy (see Figure 13) as follows:

> **21.** Where a person operates a source of energy as a switched alternative to a distributor's network, he shall ensure that that source of energy cannot operate in parallel with that network and where the source of energy is part of a low voltage consumer's installation, that installation shall comply with British Standard Requirements.

The requirements for parallel operation are much more onerous.

13.11 Safety services

56 Where an exhibition is held within a building, it is assumed that the emergency lighting and/or fire safety systems etc. will be part of the permanent installation within that building. Care should be taken to ensure that existing emergency escape signs and escape routes are not obscured, impeded or blocked.

Additional emergency lighting should be installed in those areas not covered by the permanent installation. Where an exhibition is constructed out-of-doors, an adequate fire alarm system should be installed to enclosed areas to facilitate emergency evacuation.

Where an event is taking place out-of-doors and is open to the public in partial or total darkness, then :
- emergency lighting should be provided to escape routes
- provisions should be made to ensure that alternative sources of supply for general lighting sufficient for safe evacuation, are available throughout the area.

13.12 Inspection and testing

The electrical installation of stands should be re-tested on site in accordance with Part 7 of BS 7671, after each assembly.

Users (e.g. exhibitions and stall holders) should be recommended to visually check electrical equipment for damage on a daily basis.

Chapter 14
Floor and ceiling heating systems

14.1 Scope

The recommendations in this chapter are based on the requirements of IEC standard 364.7.753. They apply to the installation of electric floor and ceiling heating systems which are erected both as thermal storage or direct acting heating systems.

14.2 The special circumstances

The risks associated with ceiling heating systems are generally that of penetration of the heating element by nails, drawing pins, etc pushed through the ceiling surface. For this reason supplementary protection against direct contact is required by the use of a 30 mA RCD.

Similarly, there are concerns that under floorheating installations can be damaged by carpet gripper nails, etc and for similar reasons protection by a 30 mA RCD or electrical separation is required.

To protect the building structure and provide precautions against fire, there are requirements to avoid overheating of the floor or ceiling heating system.

14.3 Protection against electric shock

Protection by obstacles, placing out of reach, non-conducting location and earth free local equipotential bonding are not applicable.

Protection by electrical separation is allowed if it is applied in accordance with Regulation 413-06-02(i) i.e. an isolating transformer to BS 3535 is provided for each circuit. (Note, BS 3535 is being replaced by the BS EN 61558 series of standards.)   413-06-02(i)

14.4 Supplementary protection against direct contact

Supplementary protection against direct contact is required by installation of a 30 mA RCD in accordance with Regulation 412-06-02.   412-06-02

14.5 Protection against overheating

Heating units

To avoid overheating of floor or ceiling heating systems in buildings at least one of the following measures shall be applied to limit the temperature and the heating zone to a maximum of 80 °C:

(i)   Appropriate design of the heating system

(ii)   Appropriate installation of the heating system

(iii)   Use of protective devices.

Heating units shall be connected to the electrical installation via cold leads or terminal fittings.

Heating units shall be separately connected to the cold leads e.g. by welding, brazing or by compression jointing techniques.

Heating units shall not cross expansion joints.

14.6 Standards

Flexible sheet heating elements should comply with IEC 60335-2-96 and heating cables shall comply with either IEC 60800 or for industrial applications with IEC 61423.

14.7 External influences

Heating units for installation in ceilings shall be at least IPX1 and heating units for installation in floors, of concrete or similar materials, shall be IPX7.

14.8 Identification

The installer shall provide a plan for each heating system containing the following details:

(i)   Type of heating unit

(ii)   Number of heating units installed

(iii)   Length/area of heating units

(iv)   Surface power density

(v)   Layout of the heating units

(vi)   Depth of heating unit

(vii)   Position of junction boxes

(viii) Conductors, shields and the like

(ix)   Installed/heated area

(x)   Rated voltage

(xi)   Rated resistance (cold) of the heating units

(xii)   Rated current of overcurrent protective devices

(xiii) Rated residual operating current of RCD

(xiv) The plan shall be fixed on/or adjacent to the switchgear assembly of the heating system.

Section 14.11 describes advice to be provided by the installer for the user of the installation.

14.9 Wiring systems

Heating-free areas

It may be necessary to provide areas of floor or ceiling that are unheated e.g. where fixtures to the floor or ceiling would prevent the proper emission of heat.

Account shall be taken of the increase in temperature and of its effect upon the cables, including cold leads (circuit wiring) and control wiring installed in heated zones.

The installer shall advise the client and all other contractors that no penetrating means such as screws, rivets, nails, etc shall be used in an area where floor or ceiling heaters are being installed, see 14.11.

14.10 Bathrooms and swimming pools

601-09-04

Where underfloor heating systems are installed in bathrooms and swimming pools supplied at voltages other than SELV, then the heating element should be provided either with a metallic sheath or screen overall or a metallic grid positioned above the heating elements. The screen or grid shall be connected to the supplementary bonding and earthing for the facility. In addition, the supply to the heating elements should be controlled via an RCD with a trip rating not exceeding 30 mA with no adjustable time delay.

As such facilities are likely to suffer from the ingress of water via tiling etc. and also from corrosion, provision for ready access to all terminations to permit the thorough testing of such installations is vital. The use of suitable plastic materials for enclosures and conduit/trunking etc. is one method of minimising potential corrosion effects. Furthermore, regular visual inspection of these installations, particularly in swimming pools where corrosion from the chemicals is more likely, should be carried out and adequate records kept.

14.11 Information from the contractor for the user of the installation

A description of the heating system shall be provided by the installer of the heating system for the owner of the building upon completion of the installation or for his agent.

The description shall contain at least the following information:
  a) description of the construction of the heating system, especially the installation depth from finished floor level of the floor heating units;
  b) location diagram with information concerning
   • the distribution of the heating circuits and their rated power,
   • the position of the heating units in each room,
   • particularities which have been taken into account when installing the heating units, e.g. heating-free areas, complementary heating zones, unheated areas for fixing means penetrating into the floor covering;
  c) data on the control equipment used with relevant circuit diagrams and the dimensioned position of floor temperature and weather conditions sensors, if any;
  d) data on the type of heating units and their maximum operating temperature.

The installer shall inform the owner that the description of the heating system includes all necessary information, e.g. for repair work. In addition, the owner shall be requested to hand over in time the instructions for use of the heating installation.

The installer of the heating system shall hand over an appropriate number of instructions for use to the owner or his agent upon completion. One copy of the instructions for use shall be permanently fixed in or near each relevant distribution board.

The instructions for use shall include at least the following data:

- description of the heating system and its function;
- operation of the heating installation in the first heating period in case of a new building, e.g. regarding drying out;
- operation of the control equipment for the heating system in the dwell area and the complementary heating zones as well, if any;
- information on the restriction on placing of furniture or similar;
  - additional floor coverings, e.g. carpets with a thickness of >10 mm, may lead to higher floor temperatures which can adversely affect the performance of the heating system;
  - pieces of furniture solidly covering the floor and/or built-in cupboards shall only be placed on heating-free areas;
  - furniture, such as carpets, seating and rest furniture with pelmets, which in part do not solidly cover the floor may not be placed in complementary heating zones, if any;
- in the case of ceiling heating systems, restrictions regarding the height of furniture. Cupboards of room height may be placed only below the area of ceiling where no heating elements are installed;
- dimensioned position of complementary heating zones and placing area;
- statement that in case of thermal floor and ceiling heating systems no fixing shall be made into the floor and ceiling respectively. Excluded from this requirement are unheated areas. Alternatives shall be given, where applicable.

Chapter 15
Extra-low voltage lighting installations

IEC
60364-7-715

15.1 Scope

The recommendations are based on draft CENELEC standard prHD 384.7.715 and IEC 364.7.715.

The particular requirements of this part apply to extra-low voltage lighting installations supplied from sources with a maximum rated voltage of 50 V a.c. rms or 120 V d.c.

15.2 Protection against both direct and indirect contact

For extra-low voltage lighting installations only SELV systems should be used. Where bare conductors are used (see 15.9), the maximum voltage shall be 25 V a.c. or 60V d.c. in accordance with Regulation 411-02-09.

411-02-09

Safety isolating transformers shall conform with BS 3535. (See also BS EN 61558-2-6)

The SELV sources shall be fixed.

Parallel operation of transformers in the secondary circuit is allowed only if they are also paralleled in the primary circuit and the transformers have identical electrical characteristics. See Figure 15.

Fig 15 SELV lighting installation with parallel operation of transformers and insulated conductors

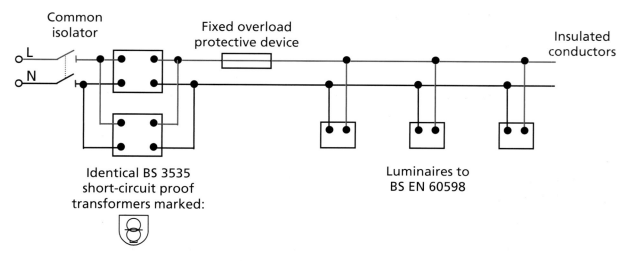

15.3 Protection against overcurrent

The SELV circuit must be protected against overcurrent either by a common protective device or a protective device for each SELV circuit, in accordance with the requirements of Chapter 43.

Chap 43

When selecting the protective device for the primary circuit account should be taken of the magnetising current of the transformer.

The overcurrent protective device shall be of the non-self-resetting type.

15.4 Isolation and switching

Where transformers are operated in parallel the primary circuit must be permanently connected to a common isolating device. See Fig 15.

15.5 Protection against fire

422

Extra-low voltage lamps and their transformers generate heat; fire risks arise from the installation of lamps close to floorboards or joists and the installation of transformers in high ambient temperatures and with limited ventilation.

Nature of processed or stored materials

The manufacturer's installation instructions must be followed, particularly those relating to mounting on flammable surfaces.

Fire risk of transformers/converters

Transformers should be either:

- protected on the primary side by the protective device required for protection against fire, see 15.6
- short-circuit proof transformers (both inherently and non-inherently proof), see 15.14 for marking.

Electronic converters should comply with BS EN 61046 and with the requirements of BS EN 60598-2-23, clause 23.7.6.

NOTE: It is recommended that converters marked with the symbol $\bigtriangledown$ are used. See 15.14 for description of symbols.

15.6 Fire risk from short-circuiting of uninsulated conductors

If both circuit conductors are uninsulated, they must be either:

- provided with a special protective device complying with the requirements below, or
- systems complying with BS EN 60598-2-23 (luminaires particular requirement, ELV lighting systems for filament lamps).

15.7 Locations with risks of fire due to the nature of processed or stored materials

482-02

Precautions against the risk of fire must be taken and should include:

- continuously monitor the power demand of the luminaires;
- automatically disconnect the supply circuit within 0.3 s in the event of a short-circuit or failure which causes a power increase of more than 60 W;

- automatically disconnect while the supply circuit is operating with reduced power (for example by gating control or a regulating process or a lamp failure) if there is a failure which causes a power increase of more than 60 W;
- automatically disconnect during switching of the supply circuit if there is a failure which causes a power increase of more than 60W; and
- the special protective device shall be fail safe.

15.8 Types of wiring system

The following wiring systems should be used:
- insulated conductors in conduit to BS EN 50086 or trunking or ducting to BS EN 50085-1;
- cables;
- flexible cables or cords;
- systems for extra-low voltage lighting according to BS EN 60598-2-23;
- track systems according to BS EN 60570.

Where parts of the extra-low voltage lighting installation are accessible, the requirements of Section 423 of BS 7671 apply.

423

Metallic structural parts of buildings, for example, pipe systems or parts of furniture, shall not be used as live conductors.

Conductors shall not be used for other purposes e.g. for supporting sign plates.

15.9 Bare conductors

If the nominal voltage is less than 25 V a.c. or 60 V d.c., bare conductors may be used provided that the extra-low voltage lighting installation complies with the following requirements:
- the lighting installation is designed, installed or enclosed in such a way that the risk of a short-circuit is reduced to a minimum; and
- the conductors used have a cross-sectional area of at least 4 mm^2, for mechanical reasons; and
- the conductors or wires are not placed directly on combustible material.

Where bare conductors are suspended above combustible material a minimum clearance of 300 mm shall be maintained.

For suspended bare conductors at least one conductor and its terminals must be insulated, for that part of the circuit between the transformer and the protective device, to prevent a short-circuit.

15.10 Suspended systems

If the fixing accessory is intended to support a pendant luminaire, the accessory should be capable of carrying a mass of not less than 5 kg. If the mass of the luminaire is greater than 5 kg, the installer should ensure that the fixing means is capable of supporting its mass. The installation instructions of the manufacturer should be followed.

Termination and connection of conductors should be by screw terminals or screw-less clamping devices complying with BS EN 60998-2-1 or BS EN 60998-2-2.

Insulation piercing connectors and termination wires, with counterweights, hung over suspended conductors, should not be used.

The suspended system should be fixed to walls or ceilings by insulated distance cleats and shall be continuously accessible throughout the route.

15.11 Cross-sectional area of conductors

The minimum cross-sectional area of the extra-low voltage conductors should be:

- 1.5 mm^2 copper for the wiring systems mentioned above, but in the case of flexible cables with a maximum length of 3 m a cross-sectional area of 1 mm^2 copper may be used;
- 4 mm^2 copper in the case of suspended flexible cables or insulated conductors, for mechanical reasons.

15.12 Electrical connections

All connections including ELV connections are required to meet the enclosure requirements of 526-03. This provides some protection against overheating in the event of a poor connection.

526-03

Bare conductors must meet the requirements of paragraph 15.9 and connections must be made in a suitable accessory.

15.13 Other Equipment

Luminaires complying with BS EN 60598 should be used.

Protective devices in the extra-low voltage circuit should be integral with the current source or shall be fixed.

Protective devices should be easily accessible.

Protective devices may be located above false ceilings which are movable or easily accessible, provided that information is given about the presence and location of the device.

If the identification of a protective device for a circuit is not immediately evident, a sign or diagram (label) close to the protective device is required to identify the circuit and its purpose.

Transformers, protective devices or similar equipment mounted above false ceilings or in a similar place must be fixed to the building structure or to fixed equipment.

15.14 Equipment marking

The following marks may be found on extra-low voltage equipment:

 Short-circuit proof (inherently or non-inherently) safety isolating transformer (IEC 61558-2-6)

Luminaire with limited surface temperature

 Luminaire suitable for direct mounting on normally flammable surfaces (IEC 60598)

 Independent ballast, IEC 60417 symbol No. 5138

Converter with a temperature limitation of 110 °C.

Chapter 16
GARDENS (other than horticultural installations)

16.1 The risk

The general rules for outdoor circuits and equipment apply to all gardens. In ornamental gardens, electrical equipment such as lighting etc., may be accessible to the general public and in private (domestic) gardens electrical work may be undertaken by people with limited knowledge.

There is no specific section in Part 6 for gardens, although Section 605 agricultural and horticultural premises, provides guidance.

605

The general rules for protection against indirect contact only apply indoors, where exposed-conductive-parts and extraneous-conductive-parts are within the equipotential zone. Outdoors, there are additional requirements that would apply to gardens, including:

413-02

471-08-01

i)   reduced disconnection times for accessible (within arm's reach) fixed Class I equipment

471-08-03

ii)   socket-outlets rated at 32 A or less are to be protected by a 30 mA residual current device

471-16-01

iii)   portable equipment rated at less than 32 A and not connected through a socket-outlet to be protected by a 30 mA residual current device.

471-16-02

16.2 Buried cables

Cables should be protected against foreseeable damage, either by armouring or by suitable enclosure. Unprotected cables should not be buried direct in the ground nor should they be clipped to wooden fences, etc which may provide inadequate support and protection.

Problems arise when either ground levels are lowered so that cables have insufficient cover or when ground levels are raised so that cables which were not intended to be buried and are not suitable for burial become buried. Such problems can arise during the course of a project and the intended ground level should be formally ascertained before the cables are installed. It must be remembered that the layout of a garden can be changed totally within a few seasons and great care must be taken to route cables where they are not likely to be disturbed or damaged, e.g. around the edge of the plot and at sufficient depth.

Buried cable routes should be identified by local route markers, and recorded on drawings, and cables buried at least 450 mm (preferably deeper) below the lowest local ground level, and a route marker tape

522-06-03

laid along the cable route about 150 mm below the surface. Cables should be shielded from prolonged exposure to direct sunlight, or be of a type suitable for such exposure. Cable with a black sheath is recommended. Generally, the ultra-violet light from the sun will affect plastics and the cable manufacturer's advice should be taken. However, cables must not be so enclosed that heat dissipation is inadequate. Cables taken overhead should have a suitable rigid support or a catenary wire, or be a type suitable for such installation. See Guidance Note 1 for more information.

522-02-01
522-11-01

522-08-04

16.3 Socket-outlets

Socket-outlets that may be reasonably expected to supply portable equipment for outside use should be protected by an RCCB complying with BS EN 61008-1 or BS 4293 or RCBO complying with BS EN 61009-1 or SRCD complying with BS 7288, to reduce the risks associated with direct contact (e.g. contact with a cut flexible cable). Socket-outlets should be suitably placed to be convenient for the purpose and of a suitable IP rating e.g. IP44 or better if located outdoors.

471-16-01
471-16-02

An RCD is not required for any circuit which is protected by electrical separation or operates at SELV or reduced low voltage.

471-16-01

16.4 Fixed equipment

Fixed equipment in the garden, such as permanently fixed garden lighting, should be securely fixed with all cables buried, or supported away from the ground or paths. All-insulated Class II equipment is recommended where possible for increased safety. Decorative lighting, including 'festoon' type lighting, should be permanently fixed if regularly used, in accordance with the recommendations for temporary decorative lighting (paragraph 11.7).

522-06-03

Other fixed equipment, including pumps, etc should be installed in accordance with the manufacturer's instructions, and the general requirements of BS 7671.

16.5 Ponds

In view of the risk of accidental or intentional immersion it is recommended that the same rules should be applied to garden ponds, especially larger ones, as are applied to swimming pools. Equipment (including cables) must be suitable for the purpose and of a suitable IP rating, or be installed in a suitable enclosure. Class II equipment should be utilised where possible. Cables should be installed in ducts or conduits built into the pond structure and not allowed to lie loose around the area. All connections must be made in robust, watertight junction boxes. Equipment to IP55 or better is recommended.

602

411-02
602-04-01

Pond lighting should meet the requirement of BS EN 60598-2-16, pumps BS EN 60335-2-41, and other equipment BS EN 60335-2-55.

Chapter 17
Mobile and transportable units

17.1 Introduction

This guidance is based upon the draft CENELEC and International Electrotechnical Commission Standard IEC 364-7-717/Ed1: Requirements for special installations or locations – Mobile or transportable units. Additional guidance is offered to cover potential UK user requirements.

17.2 Scope

The term 'mobile or transportable unit' is intended to include a vehicle and/or or transportable structure in which all or part of a low voltage electrical installation is contained.

'Units' may either be 'mobile or transportable' – self-propelled or towed vehicles, or 'transportable' - cabins or transportable containers placed in situ by other means.

Examples of units within this scope are broadcasting vehicles, medical services vehicles, fire fighting appliances, mobile workshops, and construction site cabins.

Exclusions from the scope:
– transportable generating sets
– marinas and pleasure craft
– mobile machinery
– caravans and other leisure accommodation vehicles
– traction equipment of electric vehicles.

The guidance given in this section is in addition to the general requirements of BS 7671. Where other special locations such as rooms containing showers or medical locations form part of a mobile or transportable unit, the special requirements for those installations should also be taken into consideration. In this regard, particular reference should be made to Part 6 of BS 7671 and the other relevant chapters of this Guidance Note.

17.3 The risks

The risks associated with mobile and transportable units arise from:
(i) Risk of loss of connection to earth, due to use of temporary cable connections and long supply cable runs; the repeated use of cable connectors which may give rise to 'wear and tear' and the potential for mechanical damage to these parts.

(ii) Risks arising from the connection to different national and local electricity distribution networks, where unfamiliar supply characteristics and earthing arrangements are found.

(iii) Impracticality of establishing an equipotential zone external to the unit.

(iv) Open-circuit faults of the PEN conductor of PME supplies raising the potential of all metalwork (including that of the unit) to dangerous levels.

(v) Risk of shock arising from high functional currents flowing in protective conductors – usually where the unit contains substantial amounts of electronics or communications equipment.

(vi) Vibration while the vehicle or trailer is in motion, or while a transportable unit is being moved – causing faults within the unit installation.

Particular requirements to reduce these risks include:

(vii) Checking the suitability of the electricity supply before connecting the unit, see 17.4.2.

(viii) Installing an additional earth electrode when appropriate.

(ix) A regime of regular inspection and testing of connecting cables and their couplers, supported by a log-book system of record keeping.

(x) Recommended use of stranded or flexible cables of cross-sectional area 1.5 mm^2 or greater for internal wiring with the provision of additional cable supports and stranded conductors.

(xi) Recommended use of stranded or flexible cables of cross-sectional area 2.5 mm^2 or greater for cables supplying the power to mobile units.

(xii) Protection of users of equipment outside the unit by the use of 30 mA RCDs.

(xiii) The use of RCDs to provide protection against indirect contact.

(xiv) The use of electrical separation, either by means of an isolating transformer or an on-board generator.

(xv) The use of earth-free local equipotential bonding.

(xvi) Selective use of Class II enclosures.

(xvii) Clear and unambiguous labelling of units, indicating types of supply which may be connected.

(xviii) Particular attention paid to the maintenance and periodic inspection of installations.

17.4 Supplies

17.4.1 General

The use of a TN-C system is not permitted inside any unit. Regulation 8(4) of the ESQC Regulations forbids the use of combined neutral and protective conductors in a consumer's installation.

The following methods of electricity supply to the unit are considered:

(a) Connection to a low voltage generating set in accordance with 551 Section 551 of BS 7671:

Figs 17.A.1 and 17.A.2 are typical connection arrangements.

(b) Connection to a fixed electrical installation in which the protective measures are effective, that is, to a TN or TT earthing system:

Protection against indirect contact by automatic disconnection of supply using an RCD, see Fig 17.B.1.

Protection by earth-free local equipotential bonding, see Fig 17.B.2.

Protection against indirect contact by RCD with the use of transformers to provide flexibility for single and three-phase connection arrangements, see Fig 17.B.3.

Advice on PME supplies is given in 17.4.2.

(c) Connection through means (double-wound transformer) providing simple separation from a fixed electrical installation:

With an internal IT system and an earth electrode, see Fig 17.C.1.

With an internal IT system, in conjunction with an insulation monitoring device and automatic disconnection of supply after first fault, with or without an earth electrode, see Fig 17.C.2.

With an internal TN system, with or without an earth electrode, see Fig 17.C.3.

(d) Connection through means (safety isolating transformer) providing electrical separation from a fixed electrical installation, see Fig 17.D.

Notes
(i) In supply methods (a), (b) and (c) an earth electrode may be provided.
(ii) In the case of Figure 17.C.1 an earth electrode may be necessary for protective purposes (see 17.7.1).
(iii) Simple separation or electrical separation is appropriate, for example when information technology equipment is used in the unit or when reduction of electromagnetic influences is necessary.

A unit may be supplied by any method in accordance with (a), (b), (c), or (d), or by method (a) combined with one of the other methods.

The sources, means of connection or separation may be within the unit.

17.4.2 PME networks

Regulation 9(4) of the ESQC Regulations forbids a distributor's combined neutral and protective (PEN) conductor (from a PME network) being directly connected to the extraneous-conductive-parts of a caravan. For safety reasons the DTI advise that the same prohibition should apply to mobile and transportable units.

Regulation 9(4) of the ESQC Regulations relates to distributor's networks only. In most cases mobile and transportable units, such as outside broadcast vehicles, would be connected to consumers' installations, in which case the governing legislation would be the Electricity at Work Regulations 1989, in particular regulations 8 and 9. These two regulations require precautions to be taken to prevent danger arising as a result of a fault in the distributor's network, in particular networks with a combined neutral and protective (PEN) conductor, that is PME, networks. A particular precaution required by BS 7671 is main bonding to all incoming services. Another precaution that can be taken is the connection of earth electrodes to the main earthing terminal, e.g. underground structural steelwork, water pipes, earth rods or pins. This may be achieved as a consequence of main bonding or by installing additional earth rods and/or tapes.

When mobile units are manned by electrically competent persons, those persons may be required to confirm the adequacy of the earthing of the installation to which the unit is to be connected. Otherwise the site will need to be checked in advance. Where an electricity supply is provided solely for the use of mobile units, say at a pole mounted box at a show ground or race course, earth electrodes will need to be installed as permanent features of the supply.

17.5 Protection against direct contact – protective measures

Protection by placing out of reach is not a permitted protective measure. 471-07-01

Additional protection by the use of RCDs with a rated residual operating current not exceeding 30 mA is necessary for all sockets-outlets intended to supply current-using equipment outside the unit. This requirement does not apply to socket-outlets which are supplied from circuits protected by SELV, PELV or electrical separation. 471-16-01

471-16-02

17.6 Protection against indirect contact – protective measures

The means of connection and measures for protection against indirect contact are described and illustrated below.

17.6.1 Connection to low voltage generator

Where the electricity supply to a unit is obtained by connection to a low voltage generator - see Figures 17.A.1 and 17.A.2 - only TN and IT systems are permitted and protection against indirect contact must be by automatic disconnection of supply. 413-02

(i) In units employing a TN system and a conductive enclosure or structure, the conductive structure must be connected to the main earthing bar (and to the neutral point of the generator where a low voltage generator is used as a source of supply). Where a TN system is employed in a unit without a conductive enclosure, the exposed-conductive–parts of the equipment inside the unit must be connected to the neutral point of the generator by means of protective conductors.

(ii) In units employing an IT system and a conductive enclosure, the exposed–conductive-parts of the equipment inside the units must be connected to the conductive enclosure.

Where a conductive enclosure is not employed, then the exposed-conductive-parts inside the unit must be connected together and to the protective conductors of the unit – normally this is most effectively achieved by marshalling at the main earthing bar.

An insulation monitoring device is necessary in order to achieve automatic disconnection of supply after a first fault.

Fig 17.A.1   Connection to a Class I or Class II low voltage generating set located inside the unit,
with or without an earth electrode

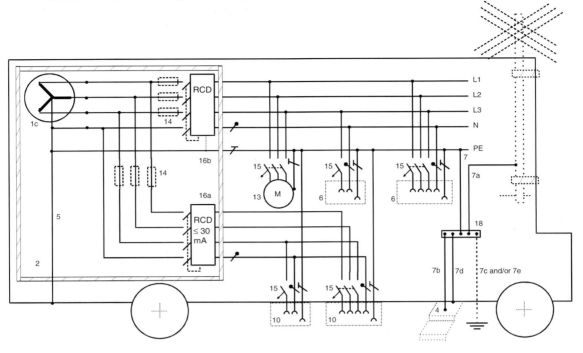

From IEC 364-7-717

Fig 17.A.2   Connection to a Class II low voltage generating set located outside the unit

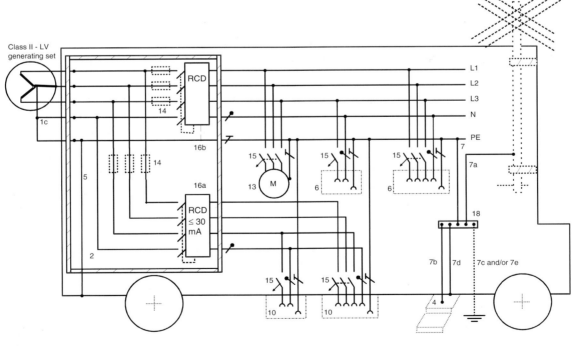

From IEC 364-7-717

Key to Figures 17.A.1 and 17.A.2

1c   Connection to LV generator set in accordance with BS 7671 Section 551-01.

2   Class II or equivalent enclosure up to the first protective device providing automatic disconnection of supply.

4   Conductive staircase, if any.

5   Connection of the neutral point to the conductive structure of the unit.

6   Socket-outlets for use exclusively in the unit.

7   Main equipotential bonding in accordance with BS 7671, Regulations 413-02 and 547-02.

7a   to an antenna pole, if any.

7b   to the conductive external stairs, if any, in contact with earth.

7c   to a functional earth electrode (in case of need).

7d   to the conductive enclosure of the unit.

7e   to an earth electrode for protective purposes, if needed.

10   Socket-outlets for current-using equipment – for use outside the unit.

13   Current-using equipment for use within the unit.

14   Overcurrent protective device, if required.

15   Overcurrent protective device e.g. one phase or phase and neutral circuit-breaker.

16a   Residual current protective device with a rated residual operating current not exceeding 30 mA, for protection by automatic disconnection of supply, of circuits of equipment for use outside the unit.

16b   Residual current protective device for protection by automatic disconnection of supply, for circuits of equipment for use inside the unit.

18   Main earthing terminal or bar.

17.6.2   Connection to a TN or TT fixed electrical installation

This section describes units for connection to a fixed electrical installation in which the protective measures are effective, that is only installations with a TN or TT earthing system. Protection against indirect contact is provided by a residual current protective device, with a rated residual operating current not exceeding 30 mA. This is not required for circuits inside units having a non-conductive enclosure where protection by earth-free local equipotential bonding is applied – see Figure 17.B.2.

Figure 17.B.1 shows the use of an on-board RCD for protection against indirect contact and a further RCD with a rated residual operating current not exceeding 30 mA, for automatic disconnection of supply for circuits for use outside the unit.

Note: For the precautions to be taken when connecting units to TN-C-S systems or PME supplies see 17.4.2.

Fig 17.B.1 Connection to a TN or TT electrical installation, with or without an earth electrode at the unit

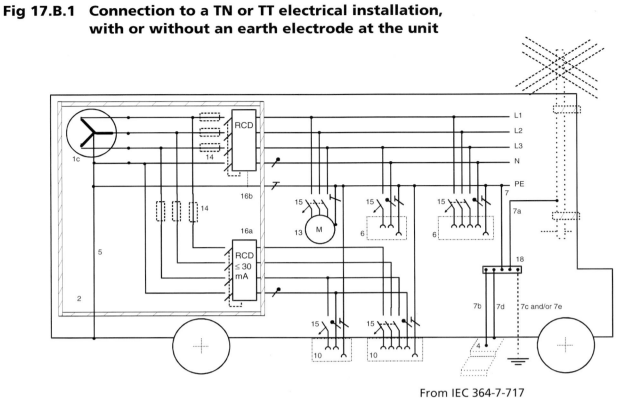

From IEC 364-7-717

Fig 17.B.2 Connection to a TN or TT electrical installation, with protection by earth free local equipotential bonding with a non-conductive enclosure in the unit

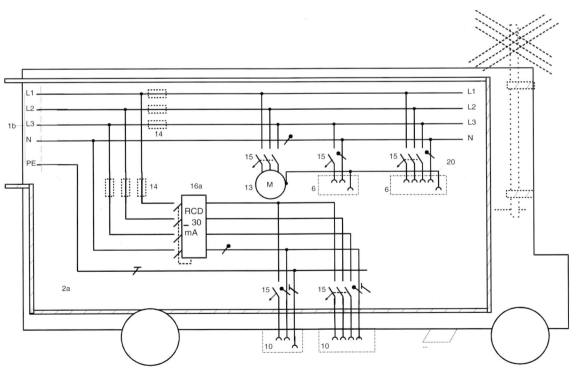

From IEC 364-7-717

Key to Figures 17.B.1 and 17.B.2

1b   Connection of the unit to a supply in which the protective measures are effective.

2   Class II or equivalent enclosure up to the first protective device providing automatic disconnection of supply.

2a   Class II or equivalent enclosure of whole internal installation of the unit.

4   Conductive staircase, if any.

6   Socket-outlets for use exclusively in the unit.

7   Main equipotential bonding in accordance with BS 7671, Regulations 413-02 and 547-02.

7a   to an antenna pole, if any.

7b   to the conductive external stairs, if any, in contact with earth.

7c   to a functional earth electrode (in case of need).

7d   to the conductive enclosure of the unit.

7e   to an earth electrode for protective purposes, if needed.

10   Socket-outlets for current-using equipment – for use outside the unit.

13   Current-using equipment for use exclusively within the unit.

14   Overcurrent protective device, if required.

15   Overcurrent protective device e.g. one phase or phase and neutral circuit-breaker.

16a   Residual current protective device with a rated residual operating current not exceeding 30 mA, for protection by automatic disconnection of supply, of circuits of equipment for use outside the unit.

16b   Residual current protective device for protection by automatic disconnection of supply, for circuits of equipment for use inside the unit.

18   Main earthing terminal or bar.

Fig 17.B.3 is a further example of the use of an RCD for indirect shock protection by automatic disconnection of supply and uses single-phase transformers, which may be connected as a three-phase unit by suitable switching. Connection of one pole of the secondary windings to the PE conductor is necessary to ensure a path for filter currents where Class I communications equipment with high protective conductor current is to be used in the unit.

As with the previous example, automatic disconnection of supply is to be provided for equipment intended to be used outside the unit. This is by an additional, separate, residual current device, with rated residual operating current not exceeding 30 mA.

This configuration is suitable where there is a reliable earth connection and where single-phase supplies only may be available. It is the configuration used for Outside Broadcast type vehicles, or other units where high protective conductor currents may reasonably be expected to be present.

By appropriate transformer connections it can be used with TT and IT sources of supply to the unit when a suitable earth electrode will be required.

Fig 17.B.3 **Connection to a single or three-phase fixed installation, suitable for TN supplies, also TT and IT supplies with an earth electrode at the unit. Transformers provide flexible connection arrangements through tapped windings and further switching (not shown)**

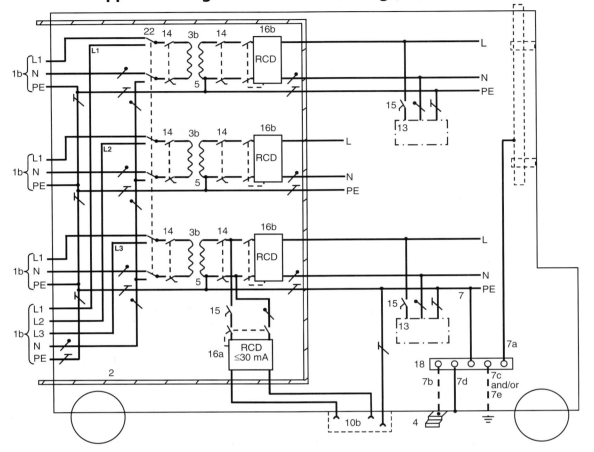

Note: For suitability of the supply see 17.4.

Key to Figure 17.B.3

1b   Connection of the unit to single or three-phase supply.

2   Class II or equivalent enclosure.

3b   Single-phase transformer.

4   Conductive staircase, if any.

5   Connection of the neutral point (or, if not available, a phase conductor) to the conductive structure of the unit.

7   Main equipotential bonding in accordance with BS 7671, Regulations 413-02 and 547-02.

7a   to an antenna pole, if any.

7b   to the conductive external stairs, if any, in contact with earth.

7c   to a functional earth electrode (in case of need).

7d   to the conductive enclosure of the unit.

7e   to an earth electrode for protective purposes, needed for TT and IT supplies to the unit.

10b   Single-phase socket outlet for current-using equipment outside the unit - BS EN 60309-2.

13   Current-using equipment for use exclusively within the unit.

14   Overcurrent protective device, if required.

15   Overcurrent protective device e.g. one phase or phase and neutral circuit-breaker.

16a Residual current protective device with a rated residual operating current not exceeding 30 mA, for protection by automatic disconnection of supply of circuits of equipment for use outside the unit.

16b Residual current protective device for protection by automatic disconnection of supply, for circuits of equipment for use inside the unit.

18 Main earthing terminal or bar.

22 Switch selecting single-phase or three-phase input connection via appropriate BS EN 60309-2 plugs.

Note Transformer primary voltage taps (switchable) and possible star/delta switching have been omitted for clarity.

17.6.3 Connection to a fixed electrical installation with any type of earthing, through a transformer providing simple separation

These arrangements are suitable for connection to a source of supply from any installation, whatever the earthing system, or lack of earthing. Simple separation is provided by a double-wound transformer, not an autotransformer. Three examples are provided:

Internal IT with an earth electrode, see Fig 17.C.1.

Internal IT system with insulation monitoring and disconnection of supply after first fault with or without earth electrode, see Fig 17.C.2.

Internal TN with or without earth electrode, see Fig 17.C.3.

Fig 17.C.1 Connection to a fixed electrical installation with any type of earthing system, (using a simple separation transformer and an internal IT system with an earth electrode)

Note, for C.1 the earth electrode is <u>not</u> optional.

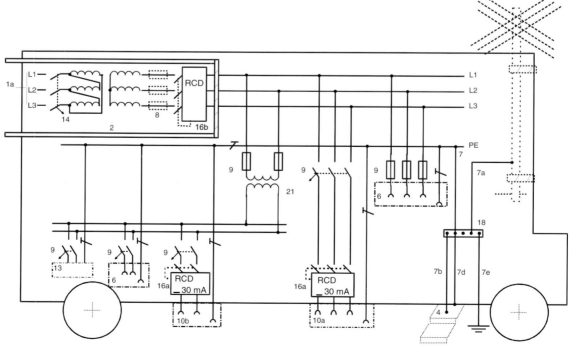

From IEC 364-7-717

Fig 17.C.2   Connection to a fixed electrical installation with any type of earthing system (using simple separation and an internal IT system with an insulation monitoring device and disconnection of supply after first fault, with or without an earth electrode)

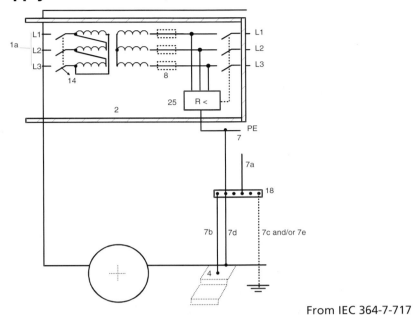

From IEC 364-7-717

Fig 17.C.3   Connection to a fixed electrical installation with any type of earthing system (using simple separation and an internal TN system, with or without an earth electrode)

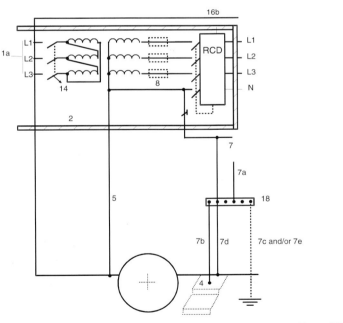

From IEC 364-7-717

Key to Figures 17.C.1 to 17.C.3

1a   Connection of the unit to a source of supply through a transformer with simple separation.

2   Class II or equivalent enclosure up to the first protective device providing automatic disconnection of supply (see item 8 or 9).

4   Conductive staircase, if any.

6   Socket-outlets for use exclusively in the unit.

7   Main equipotential bonding in accordance with BS 7671, Regulations 413-02 and 547-02.

7a   to an antenna pole, if any.

7b   to the conductive external stairs, if any, in contact with earth.

7c   to a functional earth electrode (in case of need).

7d   to the conductive enclosure of the unit.

7e   to an earth electrode for protective purposes.

8, 9   Protective devices, if required, for overcurrent and/or for protection by disconnection of supply in case of a second fault.

10a   Three-phase socket-outlet for current-using equipment outside the unit - BS EN 60309-2.

10b   Single-phase socket-outlet for current-using equipment outside the unit - BS EN 60309-2.

13   Current-using equipment for use exclusively within the unit.

14   Overcurrent protective device, if required.

16a   Residual current protective device with a rated residual operating current not exceeding 30 mA, for protection by automatic disconnection of supply, of circuits of equipment for use outside the unit.

16b   Residual current protective device for protection by automatic disconnection of supply, for circuits of equipment for use inside the unit.

18   Main earthing terminal or bar.

21   Transformer for e.g. 230 V current-using equipment.

25   Insulation monitoring device.

17.6.4 Connection to a fixed installation via a transformer providing electrical separation

The electrical separation must be achieved by the use of a safety isolating transformer (i.e. to BS 3535), see paragraph 17.7.5 and Fig 17D.

Fig 17.D **Connection to a fixed electrical installation with any type of earthing system using electrical separation provided by an isolating transformer – see 17.7.5**

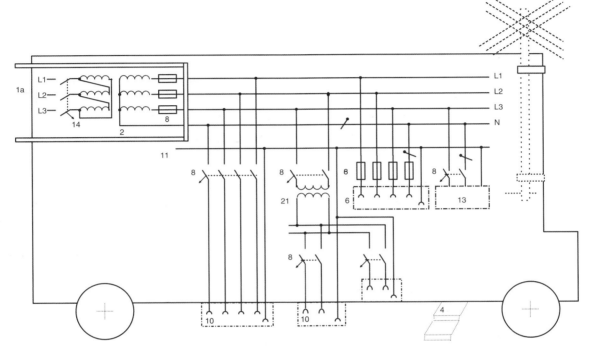

Key to Figure 17.D   From IEC 364-7-717

1a Connection of the unit to a supply through a transformer with electrical separation.

2   Class II or equivalent enclosure up to the first protective device providing automatic disconnection of supply (see item 8) .

4   Conductive staircase, if any.

6   Socket-outlets for use exclusively in the unit.

8   Protective devices, if required, for overcurrent and/or for protection by disconnection of supply in case of a second fault.

10 Socket-outlets for current-using equipment – for use outside the unit.

11 Insulated equipotential bonding in accordance with BS 7671, Regulation 413-06-05.

13 Current-using equipment for use exclusively within the unit.

14 Overcurrent protective device, if required.

21 Transformer for e.g. 230 V current-using equipment.

17.7 Internal supply system

17.7.1   IT systems

In the case of use of an internal IT system in units with a conductive enclosure, a connection of the exposed-conductive-parts of the equipment to the conductive enclosure is necessary.

In the case of units without a conductive enclosure, the exposed-conductive-parts inside shall be connected to one another and to a protective conductor.

An IT system can be provided by:

(a) an isolating transformer or a low voltage generating set, with an insulation monitoring device installed;

(b) a transformer providing simple separation that is double-wound e.g. in accordance with IEC 61558-1, only where:

- an insulation monitoring device is installed with or without an earth electrode, providing automatic disconnection of the supply in case of a first fault between live parts and the frame of the unit – see Figure 17.C.2, or

- a residual current device and an earth electrode are installed to provide automatic disconnection in the case of failure in the transformer providing the simple separation – see Figure 17.C.1. Each equipment used outside the unit shall be protected by a separate residual current protective device with rated residual operating current not exceeding 30 mA.

17.7.2   TN system

When a TN system is used in a unit with a conductive enclosure and supplied according to 17.4.1(a) a generating set or 17.4.1(c) simple separation, the conducting enclosure shall be connected to the neutral point or, if not available, a phase conductor – see Figures 17.A.1, 17.A.2 and 17.C.3.

When a TN system is used in a unit without a conductive enclosure, the exposed-conductive-parts of the equipment inside the unit shall be connected by means of a protective conductor to the neutral point or, if not available, to a live conductor.

17.7.3   Protection by the use of Class II equipment or equivalent insulation   413-03

This measure is not considered suitable as a sole means of protection against indirect contact unless the installation is effectively supervised in normal use. It is also not to be applied to any circuit including a socket-outlet, consequently it is unlikely to be suitable for mobile or transportable units. However, a Class II (or equivalent insulation) enclosure is required for any equipment installed between the source of supply to the unit and the protective devices providing automatic disconnection of the supply within the unit – including these protective devices themselves. This is shown as item 2 in the examples Figures 17.A to D.

17.7.4   Protection by earth-free local equipotential bonding 471-11

Figure 17.B.2 shows connections for a unit with protection against indirect contact provided by earth-free local equipotential bonding.

It will be seen that there is a practical difficulty in maintaining the earth-free equipotential zone in relation to any access staircase. A fundamental requirement of this protective measure is that the equipotential bonding conductors are not connected to earth – either intentionally or fortuitously. The access staircase must therefore be insulated (or isolated) from both the local equipotential bonding conductors and earth. Furthermore, it must not be possible for persons to touch the local earth-free bonding conductors from outside the unit, or vice versa.

Note   BS 7671 requires that this measure should only be applied in special situations which 471-11 are earth free and which are under 'effective supervision'. Specifiers and designers should therefore consider the circumstances of use of such units and the likelihood of appropriate supervisory measures remaining in place throughout the unit service life.

17.7.5   Protection by electrical separation

There are particular requirements for electrical separation in Regulations 413-06, 471-12 and 471-14-05 which must be complied with. Figure 17.D gives an example of a unit with protection against indirect contact by electrical separation.

If the safety isolating transformer supplies more than one item of equipment, as will be the case, Regulation 413-06-05 imposes important requirements.

17.8   Identification and labelling

A permanent notice shall be fixed to the unit in a prominent position, preferably adjacent to the supply inlet connector. The notice should state in clear and unambiguous terms the following information:

-   The type of supply which may be connected to the unit.
    Note   The descriptions used in Section 17.4 should be used as the basis for this.

-   The voltage rating of the unit.

-   The number of phases and their configuration.

-   The on-board earthing arrangement.

-   The maximum power requirement of the unit.

17.9   Wiring systems

The following wiring systems may be used.

-   Connecting cable

Flexible copper cables according to BS 7919 should be used (harmonised codes H07BB-F, H07RN-F, H07BN4-F). The minimum cable size used should be 2.5 mm^2.

The flexible cable must enter the unit by an insulating inlet in such a way as to minimize the possibility of cable damage or fault which might energise the exposed-conductive-parts of the unit. The cable sheath should be firmly gripped by the connector or anchored to the unit, to ensure stress does not bear on the connector contacts.

- Internal unit wiring

In view of the fact that some movement of wiring systems is inevitable on mobile and transportable units, internal wiring should be flexible quality.

Where wiring is to be in conduit systems, then PVC insulated cable to BS 6004 Table 4B should be used (harmonised code H07V-K).

Where wiring is to be carried out using PVC sheathed cable then PVC/PVC cable to BS 6500 (harmonised code H0VV-F) should be used.

Green/yellow bonding conductors and earthing leads should be finely stranded flexible cable to BS 6004 Table 4B (harmonised code H07V-K).

ELV dc wiring systems are outside the scope of these notes for guidance.

17.10 Main equipotential bonding

Accessible conductive parts of the unit, such as the chassis, body structure or tube systems, shall be interconnected and connected through the equipotential bonding conductors to the protective conductor of the TT, IT or TN systems within the unit. The specification of main equipotential bonding conductors shall be finely stranded flexible cable to BS 6004 Table 4B (harmonised code H07V-K, as above).

17.11 Plugs and sockets

- Plugs and sockets shall be to BS EN 60309-1.

- pin configurations shall be to BS EN 60309-2.

- plug and socket-outlet enclosures connecting the unit to the supply shall be of an insulating material and if mounted outside must have an Index of Protection not less than IP44.

Note The Index of Protection IP44 gives protection against ingress of moisture from water splashing from any direction and ingress of solid foreign objects of 1.0 mm and greater. For socket–outlets outside the unit (e.g. for supplies to equipment outside the unit) the degree of protection should be not less than IP 54.

17.12 General notes

(a) Routine maintenance and testing

The service duty of mobile and transportable units will vary with the type of unit and type of use (for example owner-operator or hire) but it is likely that frequent connecting and disconnecting combined with transporting will amount to the equivalent of rough service life. Frequency of use should therefore be an important factor in determining inspection and testing intervals. It is recommended that a visual inspection is carried out on the connecting cable and all plugs and socket-outlets before each and every transported use of the unit. The results of the visual inspection should be entered in a log-book as a permanent record of the condition of the electrical equipment. No repairs or extensions are acceptable on the external cable system and this should be replaced in its entirety if there are signs of damage or wear-and-tear.

As a minimum, the unit electrical system should be inspected and tested annually, a report obtained on its condition and the necessary maintenance work implemented. The recommendations of Part 7 of BS 7671 should be followed in this regard, together with the specific guidance given in IEE Guidance Note 3. If the unit duty is considered to be arduous, the inspection intervals should be reduced to cater for the particular conditions experienced.

All RCDs should be tested regularly by operating the test button and periodically by a proprietary instrument to ensure they conform to the parameters of BS 4293, BS EN 61008 etc as appropriate.

All tests should be tabulated for record purposes. The necessary forms required by Chapter 74 of BS 7671 must be provided to the person ordering the work, by the contractor or persons carrying out the inspection and tests.

(b) RCDs

In order to reliably prevent a fault on the equipment to be used outside the unit causing operation of the main RCD, the main RCD should incorporate a time delay (S type). Where the installations are operated and monitored by competent persons, circuit-breakers incorporating residual current protection (CBRs) with adjustable time delays to BS EN 60947/2 Annex B may be installed.

Chapter 18
Small-scale embedded generators (SSEG)

18.1 Introduction and the law

Within the lifetime of this edition of Guidance Note 7 the use of small-scale embedded generators (SSEGs) is likely to become widespread. The Electricity Safety, Quality and Continuity Regulations 2002 exempt sources of energy with an electrical output not exceeding 16 A per phase at low voltage (230 V) from Regulations 22(1)b and 22(1)d of the Regulations, and this Chapter covers such sources of energy.

The requirements for such small generators in Regulation 22(2) are:

(b) the source of energy is configured to disconnect itself electrically from the parallel connection when the distributor's equipment disconnects the supply of electricity to the consumer's installation, and

(c) the person installing the equipment ensures that the distributor is advised of the intention to use the source of energy in parallel with the network before or at the time of commissioning the source.

The requirements that are still required to be met are:

Regulation 22(1): No person shall operate a source of energy which may be connected in parallel with a distributor's network unless he-

(a) has the necessary and appropriate plant and equipment to prevent danger or interference with that network or with the supply to other consumers so far as reasonable practicable; and

(c) for low voltage installations, complies with the provisions of the British Standard Requirements.

The British Standard requirements are BS 7671 and the Section specific to generators is 551: Generating sets.

551

The equipment should be type-tested and approved by a recognised body.

18.2 Engineering Recommendation G83

To assist network operators and installers the Electricity Association has prepared Engineering Recommendation G83: Recommendations for the connection of small-scale embedded generators (up to 16 A per phase at low voltage {230 V}) in parallel with public low voltage distribution networks. The guidance given in this Chapter is intended to reproduce the requirements of the Engineering Recommendation as they would apply to persons responsible for electrically connecting such generators.

The Engineering Recommendation is for all small-scale embedded generator (SSEG)installations with an output up to 16 A including:

- Domestic combined heat and power
- Hydro
- Wind power
- Photovoltaic
- Fuel Cells.

Requirements for photovoltaic installations are found in Chapter 12 of this Guidance Note.

Engineering Recommendation G83 incorporates forms, which define the information which is required by a public Distribution Network Operator for a small-scale embedded generator which is connected in parallel with a public low voltage distribution network. Supply of information in this form, for a suitably type-tested unit, is intended to satisfy the legal requirements of the Distribution Network Operator and hence will satisfy the legal requirements of the Electricity Safety, Quality and Continuity Regulations 2002.

18.3 Installation and Wiring

The installation that connects the embedded generator to the supply terminals shall comply with BS 7671.

A suitably rated overcurrent protective device shall protect the wiring between the electricity supply terminals and the embedded generator.

The SSEG shall be connected directly to a local isolating switch. For single-phase machines the phase and neutral are to be isolated and for multi-phase machines all phases and neutral are to be isolated. In all instances the switch, which must be manual, shall be capable of being secured in the 'off' isolating position. The switch is to be located in an accessible position in the customer's installation. See Figure 18.1.

Fig 18.1   Isolation of the SSEG

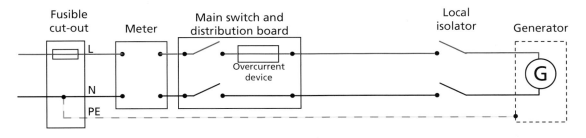

551-07-04 Means shall be provided to enable the generating set to be isolated from the public supply. The means of isolation shall be accessible to the supplier at all times.

This means of isolation from the public supply is likely to have to be an additional switch to the generator isolator discussed above in 18.3. Electricity distribution network operators are understood to be prepared to accept the distribution cut-out (fused unit) as the means of isolation.

18.5 Earthing

When a SSEG is operating in parallel with a distributor's network, there shall be no direct connection between the generator winding (or pole of the primary energy source in the case of the PV array or fuel cell) and the network operator's earth terminal. See Figure 18.2.

Fig 18.2 Earthing of parallel operation SSEG

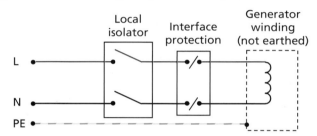

For all connections earthing arrangements shall comply with the requirements of BS 7671.

18.6 Labelling

Labels are required at the:

supply terminals (fused cut-out),

meter position,

consumer unit, and

at all the points of isolation

to indicate the presence of the SSEG within the premises. The Health and Safety (Safety Signs and Signals) Regulations 1996 stipulate that the labels should display the prescribed triangular shape and size using black on yellow colouring. A typical label both for size and content is shown below in Figure 18.3.

Fig 18.3 Earthing of parallel operation SSEG

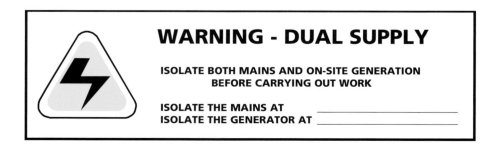

In addition, the Engineering Recommendation requires up-to-date information to be displayed at the point of connection with a distributor's network as follows:

(a) A circuit diagram showing the relationship between the embedded generator and the network operator's fused cutout. This diagram is also required to show by whom the generator is owned and maintained;

(b) A summary of the protection's separate settings incorporated within the equipment.

Figure 18.4 is an example of the type of circuit diagram that needs to be displayed. This diagram is for illustrative purposes and not intended to be fully descriptive.

Fig 18.4 Example of circuit diagram for an SSEG installation
from Engineering Recommendation G83

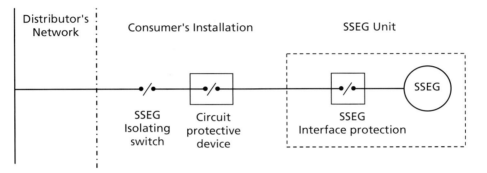

The installer is required to advise that it is the user's responsibility to ensure that this safety information is kept up to date. The installation operating instructions shall contain the manufacturer's contact details e.g. name, telephone number and web address.

18.7 Types of SSEG

(a) Domestic combined heat and power

Annex B of Engineering Recommendation G83 specifies the particular requirements for combined heating and power sets. These are likely to be the most common type of set encountered by the electricity installer. They can be incorporated into a household gas boiler to generate electricity.

Most small combined heat and power generators embody a Stirling Engine – see Figure 18.5.

Fig 18.5 Stirling Engine

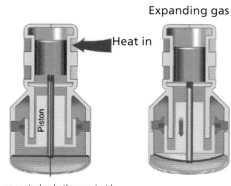

Expanding gas

Heat in

Piston

Displacer controls whether gas inside the chamber is being heated or cooled, hence whether expanding or contracting.

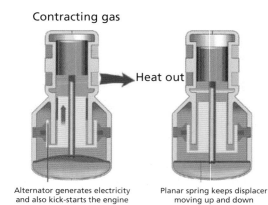

Contracting gas

Heat out

Alternator generates electricity and also kick-starts the engine

Planar spring keeps displacer moving up and down

The Stirling Engine does not burn the gas within the cylinder as in an internal combustion engine. The power to the engine is delivered by the combustion gases from the gas burner and the energy transfer is in effect achieved by the temperature difference between the burner exhaust gases and burner input air or circulating water.

The basic principle is that the sealed gas within the engine is heated by the burner gases and expands. On expansion the driven piston generates electricity in the winding and compresses the planar spring. In the expanded, say, down position of the piston the gas within the piston is subject to the cooling effect of the cooler input air (or circulated water) and contracts, assisted by the planar spring. At the compression position the gas in the cylinder is now heated by the burner gases only and is not subject to the cooling effects of the input air.

(b) Solar photovoltaic power supply systems

Chapter 12 of this Guidance Note reproduces the requirement in the draft IEC Standard for solar photovoltaic power systems. The requirements are for power photovoltaic systems that will generate only when run in parallel with the electricity supply. Requirements for photovoltaic power supply systems which are intended for stand-alone operation are under consideration by the IEC and not considered here.

Index

NOTES

NOTES

NOTES